P9-CJX-633

The Flavors of
BON APPÉTIT

The Flavors of BON APPÉTIT 2000

from the Editors of Bon Appétit

Condé Nast Books ❖ Clarkson Potter/Publishers

New York

Produced in association with Patrick Filley Associates, Inc.
Designed by Laura Hammond Hough and Jan Derevjanik

Facing Page: Top: Deviled Eggs with Curry (page 12);
Middle: Tuna, Tomato, Olive and Artichoke Sandwiches (page 85);
Bottom: Fresh Fruit with Rose Water Syrup (page 162).

Published by Clarkson Potter/Publishers, 201 East 50th Street, New York, New York 10022.
Member of the Crown Publishing Group.
Random House, Inc.
New York, Toronto, London, Sydney, Auckland

CLARKSON N. POTTER, POTTER, and colophon are
registered trademarks of Random House, Inc.

Printed in the United States of America

Library of Congress Cataloging-in-Publication Data is available upon request.

ISBN 0-609-60714-6

2 4 6 8 9 7 5 3 1

FIRST EDITION

Condé Nast Web Address: http://www.epicurious.com
Random House Web Address: http://www.randomhouse.com

contents

introduction

For seven years now, the January *Bon Appétit* has been our "Best of the Year" issue. In it, we set out to sum up the trends of the 12 months just past. Then we sit back and wait to see how close we came to spotting those that actually went on to become full-fledged events—culinary sea changes of a sort. When we look back to January 1999, it seems we did our jobs right. As both the century and the millennium turn, the trends we identified in that issue continue to define the way all of us cook, dine and entertain. They provide the themes you'll find recurring throughout this latest edition of *The Flavors of Bon Appétit*, a special collection of the best recipes that appeared in the magazine during the year.

Curried Chicken (page 68)

The anxiety-causing shift in our calendars, combined with the usual bustle of modern life, has led many of us to seek out foods that are both simple to make and simply comforting. No surprise, then, that "One-Dish Suppers," one of the year's top trends, continue to hold such appeal. You'll find an abundance of down-to-earth, all-inclusive recipes within these pages, from gently spicy Curried Chicken (page 68) to hearty Beef Stew with Herbed Dumplings (page

40) and Chicken, Shrimp and Sausage Paella (page 74).

In response to that growing desire for satisfying, easy-to-cook dishes, more and more delicious, top-notch convenience foods have become available in markets everywhere. A number of recipes in recent issues of the magazine have made use of these products. Flatbread Pizzas with Olives, Feta and Artichokes (page 116), for example, feature such sophisticated ingredients as sun-dried tomato- and basil-flavored feta cheese, canned tomatoes with Italian herbs and pitted Kalamata olives. And instead of time-consuming homemade pizza dough, the recipe uses pita bread or lavash as a "crust."

Flatbread Pizzas with Olives, Feta and Artichokes (page 116)

By contrast, we did find that readers were willing to forgo speed when it came to the simple pleasures of things like baking and barbecuing. Peasant-style breads, ubiquitous on restaurant tables and widely available in boutique bakeries and supermarkets alike, are especially popular. And smoking, which often requires that a cut of meat cook for the better part of a day in fragrant wood smoke, is all the rage. In response, you'll find examples of both trends here, among them Ciabatta (page 146)—Italy's crusty, chewy "slipper bread"—and Barbecued Texas Beef Brisket (page 46).

Barbecued Texas Beef Brisket (page 46)

Such down-home specialties point to another trend that seems only to gain in strength, one we referred to in the magazine as "The Greening of America." Greens such as kale and Swiss chard were once considered fare fit for only the humblest of tables. Today, in such recipes as Spicy Rice and Kale (page 131), Sautéed Swiss Chard (page 128) and Orecchiette with Greens, Goat Cheese and Raisins (page 112), they are celebrated for their robust taste and texture, not to men-

Toasted Almond Tofu Burgers (page 100)

tion the rich nutrients they provide—vitamin C, beta-carotene, iron, calcium and fiber among them.

Health consciousness, in fact, continues to be a hot topic. Every year, however, it seems to make news with a different headline. Most recently it was the migration of tofu and other soy products from Asian and vegetarian menus into the mainstream. Look to such recipes as Toasted Almond Tofu Burgers (page 100) and Banana, Honey and Soy Milk Smoothie (page 32) for delicious examples of this trend.

Of course, humankind cannot live by health food alone. Sometimes we need to splurge. That is why one story title in our trend-spotting issue proclaimed that "Fat Is Back." Mind you, we qualified that declaration with the words, "and a little bit won't hurt you." In just such a spirit of moderate self-indulgence, you'll find recipes like Fettuccine Quattro Formaggi (page 111), with its voluptuous sauce of Gorgonzola, provolone, Parmesan and goat cheeses; Rib-Eye Steaks with Béarnaise Butter (page 44); and Flourless Chocolate Cake with Chocolate Glaze (page 168).

Dark Chocolate Brownies with White Chocolate Chunks (page 192)

Speaking of desserts, we also recognized that there are certain sorts of sweets to which, trendy or not, we always remain faithful. These "Desserts We Love," as we called them, are the comforting favorites that never really go out of style. Cranberry-Apple Crisp (page 166), Spiced Peach Pie with Buttermilk Crust (page 160) and Dark Chocolate Brownies with White Chocolate Chunks (page 192) are among the year's outstanding examples.

Such homey recipes do offer real pleasure. But another enduring delight for many of us comes in discovering foods from places beyond our familiar borders. A survey of the foreign cooking styles recently explored in the magazine's pages reads like the itinerary of a round-the-world tour.

We cruised through Asia, sampling dishes along the way like Vietnamese Beef Soup with star anise (page 29) and Cod with Miso Glaze and Wasabi Mashed Potatoes (page 86). We stopped in Greece to enjoy such lively, unpretentious recipes as Red Snapper with Potatoes, Tomatoes and Red Wine (page 82) and Fresh Fruit with Rose Water Syrup (page 162). In Latin and Caribbean lands, we shared the excitement of such specialties as Chicken Breasts with Black Bean-Mango Salsa (page 77) and a refreshing Tropical Fruit Compote with Mango Sorbet (page 165). Like so many people who love good food, we found ourselves beguiled by the south of France and devoted an entire issue to Provence. The cuisine of that sun-kissed land is represented here in recipes ranging from Aioli with Vegetables (page 21) and Roast Leg of Lamb with Potatoes and Onions (page 59) to Strawberries in Red Wine (page 165).

Strawberries in Red Wine (page 165)

As world travelers often discover, however, the most welcome part of a journey is sometimes the homecoming. We returned in glorious fashion with our September 1999 issue, dedicated to "The American Century in Food." You'll find a special section with many of the issue's very best recipes beginning on page 198—proof positive that some of the most intriguing food trends await discovery no further away than your own back yard.

This page, clockwise from above: Chicken and Mushroom Quesadillas (page 22); Grilled Chicken Drummettes with Ancho-Cherry Barbecue Sauce (page 22); Grilled Bread with Arugula, Goat Cheese, Olives and Onions (page 15). Opposite, top: Chayote Soup with Lemongrass and Ginger (page 26). Opposite, bottom: Citrus Cooler (page 33).

starters

Deviled Eggs with Curry

6 large hard-boiled eggs, shelled
¼ cup mayonnaise
1 tablespoon minced green onion
¾ teaspoon curry powder
1 tablespoon minced fresh parsley
Niçois olives (optional)*

Niçois olives and curry powder enliven that old-fashioned favorite, deviled eggs. For an attractive presentation, pipe the filling into the hard-boiled egg halves using a pastry bag fitted with a star tip.

Cut hard-boiled eggs lengthwise in half. Scoop yolks into medium bowl. Mash yolks with fork. Add mayonnaise, minced green onion and curry powder; mix well. Season yolk mixture to taste with salt and pepper. Divide filling among egg halves, mounding slightly. Arrange eggs on platter. Sprinkle with minced parsley. *(Can be prepared 8 hours ahead. Cover and refrigerate.)* Garnish eggs with Niçois olives, if desired, and serve.

**Niçois olives are small brine-cured black olives available at specialty foods stores and in some supermarkets.*

6 SERVINGS

Wild Mushroom Crostini

Nonstick vegetable oil spray
4 egg roll wrappers

¼ cup purchased fat-free Caesar salad dressing
2 tablespoons minced shallots
4 teaspoons Dijon mustard
2 teaspoons water
⅛ teaspoon dried crushed red pepper
14 ounces assorted fresh wild mushrooms (such as oyster, crimini and stemmed shiitake), cut in half

1½ 3½-ounce packages enoki mushrooms, trimmed to 1½-inch lengths
⅓ cup (packed) thinly sliced arugula
4 sun-dried tomato halves (not packed in oil), soaked in hot water until tender, then drained and chopped

Baked egg roll wrappers make a crisp, low-fat base for the roasted mushroom topping. Peppery arugula and tangy sun-dried tomatoes add color and flavor.

Preheat oven to 350°F. Spray large baking sheet with nonstick oil spray. Place 1 egg roll wrapper on work surface. Using 2- to 2¼-inch-diameter cookie cutter, cut out 6 rounds from wrapper. Transfer rounds to prepared baking sheet. Repeat with remaining 3 wrappers, making 24 rounds total. Spray rounds with nonstick spray. Bake until golden, turning once, about 3 minutes per side. Cool.

Increase oven temperature to 400°F. Generously spray 2 more baking sheets with nonstick spray. Combine purchased dressing, shallots, mustard, 2 teaspoons water and crushed red pepper in large bowl; stir to blend. Transfer 1½ tablespoons dressing to small bowl and reserve. Place 14 ounces fresh wild mushrooms in large bowl with remaining dressing; toss to coat. Let stand 25 minutes.

Arrange half of mushroom mixture in single layer on each baking sheet. Season with salt and pepper. Bake until mushrooms are golden, turning mushrooms over halfway through baking, about 12 minutes. Cool slightly. Coarsely chop cooked mushrooms.

Return cooked mushrooms to large bowl. Add enoki mushrooms, arugula, tomatoes and 1½ tablespoons dressing. Toss to coat. Season with salt and pepper. *(Can be made 8 hours ahead. Store egg roll rounds airtight at room temperature. Cover and chill mushroom mixture. Bring to room temperature before serving.)*

Arrange egg roll rounds on platter. Spoon mushroom mixture onto egg roll rounds and serve.

MAKES 24

Lobster Crisps in Champagne-Dill Sauce

5 tablespoons butter, room temperature
6 gyoza (potsticker) wrappers*

1 1½- to 1¾-pound live lobster

2 cups extra-dry Champagne
2 cups water
⅓ cup chopped shallots
1 teaspoon tomato paste
¼ cup whipping cream
¾ cup thin strips fresh fennel bulb
¾ cup thin strips peeled carrots
¾ cup thinly sliced leek (white and pale green parts only)
4 teaspoons chopped fresh dill

Preheat oven to 350°F. Melt 1 tablespoon butter in small saucepan. Brush gyoza on both sides with butter. Arrange on baking sheet. Bake until golden, 8 minutes. Cool; wrap crisps airtight.

Cook lobster in large pot of boiling salted water until just cooked through, about 8 minutes. Transfer lobster to large bowl. Let stand 15 minutes. Working over bowl to catch juices, twist lobster tails and claws from body. Crack shells and carefully remove lobster meat. Cover and refrigerate lobster meat.

popping the cork

Despite the festive sound it makes, "popping" the cork from a bottle of Champagne or sparkling wine not only endangers nearby guests but also runs the risk of losing some of the bubbly. For the most proper of grand openings, follow these guidelines:

- Let the bottle stand undisturbed for at least two hours.
- Drape a large napkin or kitchen towel over the cork.
- Carefully untwist the wire cage that secures the cork.
- Rest the bottle's bottom against your hip, with the cork pointed away from you and others. While holding the cork securely in place with one hand, slowly twist the bottle with the other.
- The pressure inside the bottle will slowly push out the cork. As the cork emerges, apply gentle pressure on it to keep it from shooting out.
- When the cork is fully out, use the napkin or towel to wipe the bottle's opening and neck before pouring.

Place all lobster shells and juices in large saucepan. Add Champagne, 2 cups water, shallots and tomato paste. Simmer until liquid is reduced to 1 cup, about 1 hour. Strain liquid; return to same pan. Add cream; simmer until reduced to ⅓ cup, 6 minutes.

Melt 2 tablespoons butter in heavy large skillet over medium-low heat. Add fennel and carrots; sauté 3 minutes. Add leek and sauté until vegetables are crisp-tender, about 2 minutes. Cut lobster tail crosswise into 8 medallions. Add all lobster to skillet. Cover; cook just until heated through, about 2 minutes. Mix in 2 teaspoons dill.

Rewarm sauce over low heat. Whisk in 2 tablespoons butter and 2 teaspoons dill. Arrange crisps, lobster and vegetable mixture on 2 plates. Spoon sauce over and serve.

**Available at Asian markets and in the refrigerator section of many supermarkets. If unavailable, substitute wonton wrappers.*

2 SERVINGS

Grilled Bread with Arugula, Goat Cheese, Olives and Onions

This easy appetizer is great for a barbecue: Fresh goat cheese is spread over grilled sourdough bread, then topped with grilled red onions, arugula and olives.

- 9 ounces soft fresh goat cheese (such as Montrachet)
- 6 teaspoons grated orange peel

- 9 tablespoons olive oil
- 6 tablespoons orange juice
- 2 small red onions (about 1 pound), sliced into ¼-inch-thick rounds

- 12 4 x 2½ x ⅓-inch diagonal slices sourdough baguette
- 4 cups fresh arugula leaves, trimmed
- ¾ cup Kalamata olives or other brine-cured black olives (about 5 ounces), pitted, halved

Mix cheese and 4 teaspoons peel in small bowl. Season with salt and pepper. *(Can be made 1 day ahead. Cover and chill.)*

Prepare barbecue (medium-high heat). Whisk 6 tablespoons oil, orange juice and 2 teaspoons orange peel in 13 x 9 x 2-inch glass dish. Season dressing with salt and pepper. Add onions; turn to coat. Using metal spatula, transfer onions to grill and cook until tender and golden, turning occasionally and keeping onions intact, about 10 minutes. Return onions to dressing in dish; turn to coat. Set aside.

Brush 3 tablespoons oil over bread. Grill until golden, 2 minutes per side. Spread cheese over bread. Add arugula to dressing; toss to coat. Top bread with arugula, onions and olives.

12 SERVINGS

Pork Rib Satays with Peanut Sauce

indonesian dinner
for six

Pork Rib Satays with Peanut Sauce
(at right; pictured opposite)

Chayote Soup with Lemongrass
and Ginger
(page 26)

Grilled Chicken Breasts with
Grilled Pineapple Slices

Basmati Rice

Riesling or Asian Beer

Coconut Flan
(page 177)

- 5 large shallots, chopped
- 6 tablespoons soy sauce
- 4½ tablespoons distilled white vinegar
- 3 tablespoons (packed) minced peeled fresh ginger
- 1½ tablespoons peanut oil
- 3 garlic cloves, minced
- 1½ teaspoons ground coriander
- 1½ teaspoons (packed) brown sugar
- ¾ teaspoon cayenne pepper
- 2 pounds baby back pork ribs, cut into 4- to 5-rib sections

Assorted cut-up raw vegetables (such as carrots, cucumber, celery and cauliflower florets)
Peanut Sauce (see recipe below)

Mix first 9 ingredients in resealable plastic bag. Add ribs. Seal bag; turn to coat ribs with marinade. Chill overnight.

Preheat oven to 350°F. Line large roasting pan with long piece of foil, overlapping each short side by 10 inches. Place ribs and marinade on foil in pan. Spoon some marinade over ribs. Fold foil over, enclosing ribs loosely in foil. Bake until ribs are tender, about 1 hour 15 minutes. Cool ribs slightly. *(Can be prepared 1 day ahead. Keep ribs enclosed in foil in pan and refrigerate.)*

Prepare barbecue (medium heat) or preheat broiler. Unwrap ribs. Using tongs, transfer ribs to work surface. Cut rib sections between bones into individual ribs. If broiling, place ribs on baking sheet. Grill or broil ribs until well browned, about 3 minutes per side.

Serve ribs on platter with vegetables and Peanut Sauce.

6 SERVINGS

Peanut Sauce

- 1 cup peanut oil
- 8 ounces natural unsalted peanuts in their shells, shelled (1 cup shelled)
- 3 large shallots, thinly sliced
- 2 tablespoons (packed) minced peeled fresh ginger
- 1 garlic clove, minced
- 3 anchovy fillets, drained, minced
- 1 tablespoon (packed) brown sugar

In this tantalizing recipe, satays—the Indonesian specialty consisting of grilled meat threaded on skewers and served with peanut sauce—are reinterpreted using pork ribs with built-in "skewers." The ribs can be baked a day ahead, then grilled or broiled just before you serve them.

1½ teaspoons sambal oelek*
1 teaspoon ground coriander
1 teaspoon salt
½ teaspoon ground cumin
2¾ cups (or more) water
2 tablespoons fresh lemon juice

Line baking sheet with paper towels. Heat oil in large skillet over medium heat. Add peanuts; fry until golden brown, watching closely to avoid burning, about 3 minutes. Using slotted spoon, transfer peanuts to paper towels; drain. Cool. Finely grind peanuts in processor. Discard all but 1 tablespoon oil in skillet.

Heat oil in skillet over medium heat. Add shallots, ginger and garlic; sauté until shallots are almost tender, 3 minutes. Add anchovies and next 5 ingredients; stir 1 minute. Add 2¾ cups water; simmer until shallots are tender, 5 minutes. Add peanuts; simmer until mixture thickens slightly, 5 minutes longer. Season with salt. *(Can be made 1 day ahead. Cover; chill. Before using, rewarm over low heat, stirring occasionally and adding more water to thin sauce.)* Stir lemon juice into sauce. Serve warm.

**A very spicy ground chili paste available at Asian markets and some specialty foods stores and supermarkets.*

MAKES ABOUT 2 CUPS

Marinated Olives and Feta Cheese

Marinated Kalamata olives with feta cheese are a perfect complement to another Greek-inspired appetizer—a spread of broiled eggplant with tomatoes, onions, garlic, red wine vinegar and lemon juice (opposite; pictured at right). Serve wedges of pita bread with both starters.

- 1 cup Kalamata olives or other brine-cured black olives
- 1 cup cracked green olives
- 1 cup extra-virgin olive oil
- 6 tablespoons fresh lemon juice
- 5 garlic cloves, thinly sliced
- 2 tablespoons chopped fresh parsley
- 2 teaspoons grated lemon peel
- 1 teaspoon dried oregano
- ⅛ teaspoon dried crushed red pepper
- 10 ounces feta cheese, cut into ½-inch-thick slices

Pita bread, cut into wedges

Mix all olives, ¾ cup oil, 3 tablespoons lemon juice, garlic, parsley, lemon peel, ½ teaspoon oregano and red pepper in resealable plastic bag. Chill overnight. Place feta on platter. Drizzle with ¼ cup oil and 3 tablespoons lemon juice. Sprinkle with remaining ½ teaspoon oregano and black pepper. Chill at least 2 hours or overnight.

Place olives and marinade in serving bowl. Serve olives and feta cheese slices with pita bread wedges.

6 SERVINGS

Herbed Eggplant Spread

3	medium eggplants
⅓	cup canned diced tomatoes in juice, drained
½	cup chopped white onion
2	garlic cloves, minced
3	tablespoons plain yogurt
¼	cup red wine vinegar
3	tablespoons fresh lemon juice
6	tablespoons extra-virgin olive oil
3	tablespoons chopped fresh parsley
¾	teaspoon dried oregano

Preheat broiler. Pierce eggplants with fork. Place on baking sheet. Broil until skin is crisp, turning frequently, 25 minutes. Place on rack over rimmed sheet. Cool (liquid will drain from eggplants).

Peel skin from eggplants. Coarsely chop eggplants; place in large bowl. Add tomatoes, onion and garlic. Using electric mixer, beat 1 minute. Add yogurt; beat 1 minute. Reduce speed to low. Add vinegar and lemon juice; beat to blend. Gradually beat in oil. Mix in parsley and oregano. Cover; chill at least 2 hours or overnight.

6 SERVINGS

Zucchini Fritters

This tempting appetizer calls for the bright yellow-orange zucchini blossoms in addition to the vegetable itself. If the blossoms are difficult to find, use just zucchini slices. The results are equally delicious.

	Canola oil (for deep-frying)
1¾	cups all purpose flour
¼	cup cornstarch
1	tablespoon baking powder
1	teaspoon salt
2	cups chilled stout or dark beer
4	medium zucchini, cut diagonally into ¼-inch-thick slices
12	zucchini blossoms

Pour oil into heavy large saucepan to measure 3 inches in depth. Heat to 350°F. Mix flour, cornstarch, baking powder and salt in large bowl. Add stout. Whisk until smooth batter forms. Working in batches of 5 or 6 zucchini slices or blossoms and using tongs, dip zucchini slices and blossoms into batter and add to hot oil. Cook until golden brown, about 2 minutes per side. Using slotted spoon, transfer fritters to paper towels. Sprinkle with salt.

6 SERVINGS

Using *gyoza* (potsticker) wrappers simplifies the recipe for these Swiss chard- and ricotta-filled ravioli. They're tossed with melted butter mixed with chopped fresh sage.

Swiss Chard Ravioli

- ¼ cup water
- 1 pound Swiss chard, center spine and stems trimmed
- 1 cup ricotta cheese
- ⅓ cup freshly grated Parmesan cheese
- 1 large egg
- 1 garlic clove, minced
- 1 teaspoon chopped fresh thyme
- ¾ teaspoon salt
- ½ teaspoon chopped fresh rosemary
- ¼ teaspoon ground black pepper

- 64 gyoza (potsticker) wrappers (from two 12-ounce packages)*
- 1 large egg white, beaten to blend

- ¾ cup (1½ sticks) butter
- ¼ cup chopped fresh sage
- Additional freshly grated Parmesan cheese (optional)

Bring ¼ cup water to boil in large pot. Add chard leaves. Cover; cook until tender but still bright green, stirring occasionally, about 3 minutes. Drain. Cool slightly. Squeeze dry. Chop chard finely. Transfer to large bowl. Mix in ricotta, ⅓ cup Parmesan cheese, egg, garlic, thyme, salt, rosemary and pepper.

Line baking sheet with foil or plastic wrap; sprinkle with flour. Place 1 gyoza wrapper on work surface. Brush surface of wrapper with some egg white. Spoon generous 1 teaspoon chard mixture into center of wrapper. Top with another wrapper. Press edges together to seal. Transfer to baking sheet. Repeat with remaining wrappers, egg white and chard mixture to make 32 ravioli total.

Melt butter in heavy small skillet over medium heat. Add sage; stir 1 minute. Season with salt and pepper. Remove from heat.

Working in batches, cook ravioli in large pot of boiling salted water until just tender, stirring occasionally, about 4 minutes. Transfer to large shallow bowl. Pour sage butter over and toss. Serve, passing additional Parmesan, if desired.

*Gyoza *wrappers can be found at Asian markets and in the refrigerator section of many supermarkets. If unavailable, substitute wonton wrappers and cut into 3½-inch rounds.*

8 SERVINGS

Aioli with Vegetables

- 4 large garlic cloves, peeled
- ½ teaspoon salt

- 6 tablespoons plus ¾ cup olive oil
- ¼ cup fresh lemon juice
- 3 large egg yolks
- 1½ tablespoons water

- Steamed cut-up fresh vegetables (such as red-skinned potatoes, carrots, zucchini, fennel bulbs, cauliflower and green beans)
- 6 hard-boiled eggs, shelled, each cut into 4 wedges

Using mortar and pestle, mash garlic with salt until almost smooth. Transfer garlic mixture to processor.

Whisk 6 tablespoons oil, lemon juice, yolks and 1½ tablespoons water in small metal bowl. Set bowl over saucepan of barely simmering water (do not allow bowl to touch water). Whisk until thermometer registers 140°F for 3 consecutive minutes, about 9 minutes total. Cool slightly. Transfer to processor with garlic.

With machine running, gradually add remaining ¾ cup oil in thin steady stream and blend until thick (if oil is added too quickly, mayonnaise will separate and become runny). Season with salt and pepper. Transfer to bowl. *(Can be made 1 day ahead. Chill.)*

Place bowl of aioli on platter. Surround with steamed vegetables and hard-boiled eggs and serve.

6 SERVINGS

all about aioli

Sometimes referred to as the butter of Provence, the garlic-flavored mayonnaise known as aioli is indeed a justly popular condiment in the south of France. It is prepared the same way that mayonnaise is made, by whisking room-temperature egg yolks while slowly pouring in a thin stream of olive oil to build a thick emulsion. However, before the oil is added, a generous helping of garlic cloves is blended with the egg yolks—as many as six cloves for one cup of aioli. These days, using raw egg yolks is considered a possible health hazard, so the yolks are cooked to a safe temperature before they are incorporated into an aioli recipe like the appetizer at left.

The final, luxurious sauce may be served cold with vegetables, seafood, poultry or meat. Aioli is also added as an enrichment to soups. And, yes, it is sometimes simply spread like butter on bread.

Aioli migrated to American shores with French settlers in the region of Louisiana. There, to this day, it is sometimes called "High Holy" mayonnaise, a playful verbal twist that also reflects the esteem in which it is held.

Grilled Chicken Drummettes with Ancho-Cherry Barbecue Sauce

Dried tart cherries provide the "sweet" and *ancho* chilies the "spicy" in this sweet and spicy barbecue sauce. The dried chilies can be found at Latin American markets, specialty foods stores and some supermarkets.

- 1¼ cups apple cider vinegar
- ¾ cup ketchup
- ¾ cup chopped onion
- ¾ cup dried tart cherries
- ⅓ cup (packed) dark brown sugar
- ¼ cup water
- 3 tablespoons mild-flavored (light) molasses
- 2 large dried ancho chilies (about 1 ounce), stemmed, seeded
- 2 garlic cloves
- 1 teaspoon ground coriander
- Pinch of ground cloves
- 3 pounds chicken wing drummettes

Combine all ingredients except chicken in heavy medium saucepan. Bring to boil. Reduce heat to medium-low. Cover; simmer until chilies and cherries are tender, 20 minutes. Working in batches, puree in blender. Return to pan. If necessary, simmer uncovered until sauce is reduced to 3 cups. Season with salt and pepper.

Prepare barbecue (medium heat). Sprinkle chicken with salt and pepper. Grill until just cooked through, turning occasionally, about 10 minutes. Brush sauce over; continue grilling until glazed, turning chicken and basting often, 5 minutes. Serve with remaining sauce.

10 SERVINGS

Chicken and Mushroom Quesadillas

- ¼ cup (½ stick) butter
- 2½ teaspoons chili powder
- 2 garlic cloves, minced
- 1 teaspoon dried oregano
- 4 ounces fresh shiitake mushrooms, stemmed, sliced
- 4 ounces button mushrooms, sliced
- 1½ cups shredded cooked chicken
- ⅔ cup finely chopped onion
- ⅓ cup chopped fresh cilantro
- 2½ cups grated Monterey Jack cheese
- Olive oil
- 16 5½-inch-diameter corn tortillas

Melt butter in large skillet over medium-high heat. Add chili powder, garlic and oregano. Sauté until fragrant, about 1 minute. Add shiitake and button mushrooms and sauté until tender, about 10 minutes. Remove from heat. Mix in chicken, onion and cilantro. Cool 10 minutes. Mix in cheese. Season with salt and pepper. *(Can be made 8 hours ahead. Cover and chill.)*

Prepare barbecue (medium heat). Lightly brush oil on 1 side of 8 tortillas. Place tortillas, oil side down, on large baking sheet. Divide chicken mixture among tortillas, spreading to even thickness. Top with remaining 8 tortillas; press, then brush with oil.

Grill quesadillas until heated through and golden brown, about 3 minutes per side. Cut into wedges.

12 TO 16 SERVINGS

Asparagus and Sugar Snap Peas with Honey-Mustard Dip

1¼ pounds asparagus, trimmed
1¼ pounds sugar snap peas, trimmed

6 tablespoons Dijon mustard
⅓ cup fresh lemon juice
⅓ cup honey
¼ cup white wine vinegar
¼ cup chopped fresh dill
½ cup olive oil

Bring large pot of water to boil. Add asparagus and blanch 2 minutes. Add sugar snap peas and blanch until vegetables are crisp-tender, about 1 minute longer. Drain. Transfer to large bowl of ice water and cool. Drain vegetables; pat dry.

Mix mustard, lemon juice, honey, vinegar and dill in medium bowl. Gradually whisk in oil. Season with salt and pepper. *(Vegetables and sauce can be made 1 day ahead. Cover separately and chill. Before serving, bring dip to room temperature; rewhisk.)*

Place dip in bowl; set on platter. Surround with vegetables.

12 SERVINGS

all about asparagus

Fresh asparagus is one of springtime's most anticipated vegetables. The tender-crisp stalks are versatile, enjoyed as hot or cold appetizers, salads and side dishes. They may be cooked by boiling, steaming, microwaving, sautéing, stir-frying, deep-frying or grilling.

The most common form is slender, uniformly green stalks, though purple-tinged stalks are also available. Especially prized for its delicate taste and texture is young asparagus no thicker than a pencil. More popular in Europe, but also sometimes available in well-stocked markets, is plump white asparagus. Its color results from growing the stalks in mounds of earth to deprive them of sunlight, which prevents chlorophyll development; the taste is generally considered more robust.

Whatever type you buy, look for firm, unblemished stalks with compact tips and cut ends that do not appear too woody or dry. Cook them as soon as possible after purchase, storing them upright with the cut ends in cold water.

Spinach, Mustard Green and Potato Soup

rainy day lunch for eight

Spinach, Mustard Green and Potato Soup (at right; pictured opposite)

Grilled Ham and Cheese Sandwiches

Hot Tea or Hot Cider

Walnut-topped Spice Cookies (page 196)

- 4 tablespoons olive oil
- 2 cups chopped onions
- 2 pounds Yukon Gold potatoes, peeled, cut into 1-inch pieces
- 8 cups (or more) water
- ½ teaspoon dried crushed red pepper

- 4 garlic cloves, minced
- 1 bunch mustard greens (about 12 ounces), stems trimmed, leaves coarsely chopped
- 1 10-ounce package fresh spinach, stems trimmed

Sour cream

Heat 2 tablespoons oil in heavy large pot over medium heat. Add chopped onions and sauté until tender and golden, about 8 minutes. Add potatoes and sauté 3 minutes. Add 8 cups water and dried crushed red pepper. Bring to boil. Reduce heat. Simmer until potatoes are tender, about 20 minutes.

Meanwhile, heat remaining 2 tablespoons oil in another heavy large pot over medium heat. Add garlic; sauté until fragrant, about 1 minute. Add mustard greens and all but 1 cup spinach leaves; sauté until wilted, about 3 minutes.

Add sautéed greens to potato mixture. Working in batches, puree soup in blender until smooth. *(Can be prepared 1 day ahead. Cool. Cover and refrigerate.)* Return soup to pot. Bring to simmer, thinning with more water, if desired. Season with salt and pepper.

Cut remaining 1 cup spinach leaves into ⅓-inch-wide slices. Ladle soup into bowls. Add dollop of sour cream to each bowl. Garnish soup with sliced spinach leaves and serve.

8 SERVINGS

There's no cream in this rich-tasting soup, so go ahead and garnish it with sour cream. It's terrific paired with the Bacon and Thyme Biscuits on page 148, and can be made a day ahead for convenience.

Zucchini and Dill Soup

- 2 tablespoons (¼ stick) butter
- 5 zucchini (about 1¼ pounds), thinly sliced
- 1 large onion, chopped
- 2 garlic cloves, chopped
- 1 tablespoon chopped fresh dill
- 4 cups canned low-salt chicken broth
- Sour cream (optional)
- Additional chopped fresh dill

Melt butter in large pot over medium-high heat. Add next 4 ingredients and sauté until tender, about 10 minutes. Add broth and bring soup to boil. Reduce heat and simmer soup for 10 minutes.

Working in batches, puree soup in blender. Return soup to pot. Season with salt and pepper. Bring to simmer. Ladle into bowls. Top with sour cream, if desired. Sprinkle with dill.

6 SERVINGS

❖

Chayote Soup with Lemongrass and Ginger

- 7 cups canned low-salt chicken broth
- 1 stalk fresh lemongrass,* thinly sliced
- 1 1-inch piece fresh ginger, sliced
- 3 fresh or frozen kaffir lime leaves*
- ½ cinnamon stick
- ½ teaspoon ground nutmeg
- ¼ teaspoon cayenne pepper
- 2 chayote squash, peeled, rinsed, quartered lengthwise, cored, thinly sliced crosswise
- ¼ cup fresh lemon juice
- ¾ cup chopped fresh Italian parsley

Combine first 7 ingredients in large pot. Bring to boil. Reduce heat and simmer 10 minutes to blend flavors. Strain liquid into bowl; return to same pot. Discard solids in strainer.

Bring liquid in pot to boil. Add squash; reduce heat and simmer until squash are crisp-tender, about 7 minutes. Stir in lemon juice. Stir in parsley. Serve soup hot or chilled.

**Available at Asian markets and some specialty foods stores.*

6 SERVINGS

Low-fat buttermilk and nonfat yogurt are used in this refreshing, tangy soup, making it low in both calories and fat. Canned crabmeat makes the preparation easy.

Buttermilk Soup with Cucumber and Crab

- 3 large cucumbers (about 2½ pounds), peeled, seeded
- 1 cup low-fat (1%) buttermilk
- ½ cup plain nonfat yogurt
- ⅓ cup chopped onion
- 1¼ teaspoons ground cumin

- 8 ounces crabmeat, drained
- 1 ripe tomato, seeded, chopped
- 3 green onions, thinly sliced

Chop 2¼ cucumbers. Puree chopped cucumbers, buttermilk, yogurt, onion and cumin in blender until smooth. Season with salt and pepper. Cover; chill until very cold, at least 4 hours. *(Can be made 1 day ahead. Keep refrigerated.)*

Finely chop remaining ¾ cucumber. Mound crabmeat in center of 8 bowls, dividing equally. Ladle cold soup around crabmeat. Sprinkle with tomato, green onions and finely chopped cucumber.

8 SERVINGS

Vegetable Soup with Pistou

Pistou—a pesto from Provence made with garlic, basil and Parmesan cheese—is a delicious topping for this hearty vegetable soup. It would also be good tossed with pasta or spread on toasted baguette slices.

- 10 cups (or more) water
- 1 cup dried cannellini (white kidney beans)
- 1 large onion, chopped
- 6 garlic cloves, minced

- 1 pound small red-skinned potatoes, quartered
- 2 leeks (white and pale green parts only), thinly sliced
- 2 large carrots, peeled, chopped
- 1 14½-ounce can diced tomatoes in juice
- ½ pound green beans, trimmed, cut into 1-inch pieces
- 2 medium zucchini, chopped
- 4 fresh thyme sprigs
- 1 bay leaf

- 1 cup farfalle (bow-tie pasta)
- Pistou (see recipe below)

Combine 4 cups water, beans, onion and 2 garlic cloves in heavy large pot. Bring to boil. Reduce heat. Cover; simmer until beans are just tender, stirring occasionally, about 55 minutes.

Add 6 cups water, remaining 4 garlic cloves, potatoes, leeks, carrots, tomatoes with juices, half of green beans, half of zucchini, thyme and bay leaf. Bring to boil. Cover; simmer until vegetables are tender, stirring occasionally, 30 minutes.

Add pasta to soup. Simmer 12 minutes. Add remaining green beans and zucchini to soup. Simmer until pasta is just cooked through, about 5 minutes longer. Season to taste with salt and pepper. Ladle soup into bowls. Spoon 1 tablespoon Pistou atop each. Pass remaining Pistou separately.

6 TO 8 SERVINGS

Pistou

- 3 garlic cloves
- 3 cups (packed) fresh basil leaves
- ½ teaspoon salt
- 6 tablespoons olive oil
- ¾ cup grated Parmesan cheese

Finely chop garlic in processor. Add basil and ½ teaspoon salt. Process until basil is finely chopped, scraping down sides of bowl occasionally. With machine running, gradually blend in oil. Add cheese; process to blend well. Season with pepper. Transfer to bowl. *(Can be prepared 2 days ahead. Place plastic wrap directly onto surface of Pistou; refrigerate.)*

MAKES ABOUT ¾ CUP

Vietnamese Beef Soup

5 14½-ounce cans low-salt chicken broth
1¼ pounds meaty beef neck bones or beef shank bones
8 green onions
3 large whole star anise*

1 6-ounce package dried rice stick noodles (maifun)**
1 cup fresh cilantro leaves
1 cup fresh mint leaves
1 serrano chili, thinly sliced

1 12-ounce rib-eye steak, fat trimmed, very thinly sliced

Combine broth, beef bones, 3 green onions and star anise in heavy large pot. Bring to boil. Reduce heat, cover and simmer gently 3 hours. Remove beef bones and green onions from broth; discard. Season broth with salt and pepper.

Soak rice stick noodles in bowl filled with enough hot water to cover noodles for 3 minutes. Drain. Using scissors, cut noodles into 4-inch lengths. Slice remaining 5 green onions and place on platter. Arrange cilantro leaves, mint leaves and chili on same platter.

Bring broth to boil. Add noodles and cook until tender, about 2 minutes. Add rib-eye steak and simmer 1 minute. Ladle soup into bowls. Pass condiments separately.

**Star anise is available at Asian markets and specialty foods stores, and in the spice section of some supermarkets.*

***Dried rice stick noodles are available at Asian markets and in the Asian foods section of some supermarkets.*

4 SERVINGS

the star of asia's kitchens

Unlike most spices, star anise isn't a seed, a root or a bark. Instead, it is the dried fruit of a type of evergreen tree native to southern China, and it takes its name from its eight-pointed stellar shape and from its aromatic licorice-like flavor.

Star anise is a staple in Asian kitchens, most often combined with ground cassia (Chinese cinnamon), cloves, fennel seeds and Szechuan peppercorns in the classic Chinese seasoning known as five-spice powder. It nicely complements long-simmered or barbecued meat or poultry dishes, and may also be used much as aniseed would to flavor baked goods, custards or fruit desserts. In the recipe at left, the spice lends its unique sweet, woodsy taste to a soup with Asian overtones.

Star anise may be found whole, broken into individual "points" or ground in Asian markets. Store at cool room temperature in an airtight container.

Carrot Soup with Thyme and Fennel

- ¼ cup (½ stick) butter
- 4 medium carrots, peeled, chopped
- ¾ cup chopped onion
- ¾ cup chopped leek (white and pale green parts only)
- 2 garlic cloves, chopped
- ½ teaspoon chopped fresh thyme
- ¼ teaspoon fennel seeds
- 5 cups (or more) canned low-salt chicken broth

Additional chopped fresh thyme

Melt ¼ cup butter in large saucepan over medium-low heat. Add carrots, onion, leek, garlic, ½ teaspoon thyme and fennel seeds; stir to coat. Cover; cook until onion is translucent, stirring occasionally, about 15 minutes. Add 5 cups chicken broth. Bring to simmer. Cover soup partially and simmer until carrots are very tender, stirring occasionally, about 40 minutes. Cool slightly.

Working in batches, puree soup in blender. Return to pan. Thin to desired consistency with broth. Season with salt and pepper.

Bring soup to simmer. Ladle into bowls. Sprinkle with thyme.

4 SERVINGS

Cream of Red Bell Pepper Soup

This vegetarian soup has the rustic flavors of roasted red bell peppers, fresh garlic and olive oil. Half and half adds richness, while a splash of vinegar provides bite.

- 2½ pounds red bell peppers

- 1 tablespoon olive oil
- 1 cup chopped shallots
- 2 garlic cloves, minced
- 1 tablespoon chopped fresh thyme
- 3 cups (or more) canned vegetable broth

- ½ cup half and half
- 2 teaspoons red wine vinegar
- ⅛ teaspoon cayenne pepper

Sliced fresh basil

Char peppers over gas flame or in broiler until blackened on all sides. Enclose in paper bag and let stand 10 minutes to steam. Peel, seed and slice roasted peppers.

Heat oil in heavy large saucepan over medium heat. Add

shallots, garlic and thyme and sauté 3 minutes. Add 3 cups broth and all but 4 slices of roasted pepper. Simmer uncovered until peppers are very soft, about 20 minutes.

Working in batches, puree soup in blender until smooth. Return to same pot. Add half and half, vinegar and cayenne pepper. Rewarm soup, thinning with additional broth, if desired. Season with salt and pepper. Garnish with pepper strips and basil.

4 SERVINGS

Lentil Soup with Roasted Vegetables

- 1 1- to 1¼-pound eggplant, unpeeled, quartered lengthwise
- 4 large plum tomatoes, quartered lengthwise
- 1 large onion, cut into 8 wedges
- ½ large green bell pepper, quartered, seeded
- 4 large garlic cloves, peeled
- 2 tablespoons olive oil

- 5 cups (or more) water
- 1¼ cups dried brown lentils
- 4 teaspoons ground cumin

- ½ cup plain nonfat yogurt

Preheat oven to 450°F. Arrange first 5 ingredients on large nonstick baking sheet. Drizzle with 2 tablespoons olive oil. Roast vegetables 20 minutes. Turn vegetables over and roast until tender and brown around edges, stirring occasionally, about 20 minutes longer. Cool vegetables slightly (do not clean baking sheet).

Scoop eggplant pulp from peel into processor; discard peel. Add roasted onion and garlic to processor; puree until smooth. Transfer eggplant mixture to large saucepan. Coarsely chop tomatoes and bell pepper; combine in small bowl.

Add 1 cup water to baking sheet; stir to scrape up any browned bits. Add to saucepan with eggplant mixture. Add 4 cups water, lentils and cumin and bring to boil. Reduce heat, cover and simmer until lentils are almost tender, about 30 minutes. Mix in all but ¼ cup tomato and bell pepper mixture. Simmer uncovered until lentils are very tender, thinning with more water if soup is too thick, about 10 minutes longer. Season with salt and pepper.

Ladle soup into bowls. Drizzle large spoonful of yogurt over each. Top with remaining ¼ cup tomato and bell pepper mixture.

6 SERVINGS

good-for-you lentils

Today's health-conscious cooks are discovering a secret long cherished in kitchens as far-flung as those in France and India: Lentils, those tiny dried seeds of the legume family, are easy to cook, versatile, delicious and good for you.

Unlike dried beans, which require soaking for at least several hours before cooking, lentils—whether the brown, red, green or yellow variety—can go straight into the pot after they've been sorted (to remove any debris) and rinsed. They usually cook in less than half an hour, though they may be included in longer-cooking dishes. And, like beans, they can lend robust, earthy taste and texture to soups (like the one at left), stews and salads alike.

They also make a major contribution to good nutrition. Lentils are very high in protein and an outstanding source of fiber. In addition, they offer lots of blood-building iron along with folate, an important B vitamin believed by doctors to provide numerous health benefits.

Blended Lemon-Lime Gin Fizz

For larger parties, you can prepare several batches of this drink a few hours ahead of time and store them in the freezer. Then, before serving, thaw the mixture slightly and whisk vigorously to blend.

22 ice cubes
½ cup gin
½ cup whipping cream
½ cup club soda
¼ cup frozen lemonade concentrate
¼ cup frozen limeade concentrate
3 tablespoons frozen orange juice concentrate
3 tablespoons powdered sugar
Ground nutmeg
Lemon- and lime-peel twists
Lemon slices

Place first 8 ingredients in blender; blend until smooth. Pour into 4 glasses. Sprinkle with nutmeg. Garnish with lemon- and lime-peel twists and lemon slices; serve.

4 SERVINGS

Banana, Honey and Soy Milk Smoothie

1½ bananas, peeled, cut into ½-inch rounds, frozen
1 cup light (1%) soy milk
1 cup ice cubes
1 tablespoon honey
½ teaspoon vanilla extract

Combine all ingredients in blender. Blend until smooth. Pour smoothie into 2 glasses and serve immediately.

2 SERVINGS

❖

Good any time of day, this refreshing nonalcoholic concoction combines both orange juice and grapefruit juice, as well as fresh lime juice and lemon juice.

Citrus Cooler

- 1 cup water
- ¼ cup sugar
- 1 cup fresh orange juice
- 1 cup fresh grapefruit juice
- ¼ cup fresh lime juice
- 2 tablespoons fresh lemon juice
- Ice cubes

Stir 1 cup water and sugar in small saucepan over medium-low heat until sugar dissolves. Bring to boil. Transfer syrup to pitcher and refrigerate until cold. Add orange juice, grapefruit juice, lime juice and lemon juice to pitcher and stir to blend. *(Can be prepared 1 day ahead. Keep refrigerated.)* Fill 4 glasses with ice. Pour citrus cooler over and serve.

4 SERVINGS

Mango-Boysenberry Mimosa

2 cups frozen unsweetened boysenberries, thawed
2 tablespoons sugar

3 cups chilled orange juice (do not use freshly squeezed)
1½ cups frozen orange-peach-mango juice concentrate
1 750-ml bottle of chilled dry Champagne
10 small orange slices

Place 10 berries in freezer; reserve for garnish. Puree remaining berries in processor. Strain through sieve over bowl, pressing on solids. Mix in sugar. *(Can be made 1 day ahead. Cover; chill.)*

Whisk orange juice and concentrate in pitcher to blend. Mix in Champagne. Divide mimosa among 10 Champagne glasses. Drizzle 1½ teaspoons berry puree over each. Garnish with orange slices and reserved berries and serve.

10 SERVINGS

These three classic brunch drinks (pictured opposite)—Iced Espresso-Almond Latte (page 36), Mango-Boysenberry Mimosa (at left) and Black Currant Iced Tea with Cinnamon and Ginger (at left)—have been updated to make them a hit at any party.

Black Currant Iced Tea with Cinnamon and Ginger

6 cups water
12 wild black currant herbal tea bags
2 3-inch-long cinnamon sticks, broken in half
1 tablespoon (packed) minced peeled fresh ginger
6 tablespoons frozen raspberry-cranberry juice concentrate
¼ cup sugar

Ice cubes
8 cinnamon sticks
8 crystallized ginger rounds

Bring 6 cups water to boil in large saucepan. Add tea bags, broken cinnamon sticks and fresh ginger. Remove from heat. Cover; steep 10 minutes. Mix in concentrate and sugar. Chill until cold. Strain mixture into pitcher. *(Can be made 1 day ahead. Cover; chill.)*

Fill 8 wineglasses with ice. Pour tea mixture over. Garnish with cinnamon sticks and ginger rounds and serve.

8 SERVINGS

Iced Espresso-Almond Latte

- 2 cups plus 1 teaspoon finely ground espresso coffee beans
- 3 cups water
- 3 tablespoons golden brown sugar
- 1½ cups whole milk
- 5 teaspoons almond syrup (such as Torani)

Ice cubes
Espresso Whipped Cream (see recipe below)

Look for almond syrup in the coffee and tea section of the supermarket. The drink tastes even better topped with the accompanying whipped cream flavored with brown sugar and espresso powder.

Fill coffee filter or basket of coffeemaker with 1 cup ground espresso beans. Add 1½ cups water to coffeemaker and brew. Pour coffee into bowl. Repeat with 1 cup ground espresso beans and remaining 1½ cups water to make total of 2 cups coffee. Mix in sugar, then milk and almond syrup. Refrigerate coffee mixture until cold, at least 2 hours or overnight.

Fill 6 glasses with ice. Divide coffee mixture among glasses. Top each with whipped cream. Sprinkle with remaining 1 teaspoon ground espresso beans and serve.

6 SERVINGS

Espresso Whipped Cream

- 1 cup chilled whipping cream
- 3 tablespoons golden brown sugar
- 1 teaspoon vanilla extract
- 1 teaspoon instant espresso powder

Beat cream, brown sugar, vanilla and instant espresso powder in medium bowl to soft peaks. *(Whipped cream can be made 4 hours ahead; cover with plastic wrap and refrigerate.)*

MAKES ABOUT 2 CUPS

Hot Cocoa with Coffee Liqueur

5 cups milk
⅓ cup unsweetened cocoa powder
6 tablespoons sugar
1½ tablespoons instant coffee powder
Pinch of salt
3 ounces semisweet chocolate, chopped
¼ cup coffee liqueur

Bring first 5 ingredients to simmer in heavy large saucepan over medium heat, whisking frequently. Add chocolate; whisk until melted and smooth. Mix in liqueur. Ladle into mugs and serve.

6 SERVINGS

Southwestern Bloody Mary

Canned *chipotle* chilies spice up a classic Bloody Mary. Fresh red chilies make a festive garnish. (Begin preparations at least two hours ahead of when you want to serve the drink.)

3 cups canned vegetable juice
2 tablespoons fresh lemon juice
1 tablespoon minced fresh cilantro
1 tablespoon Worcestershire sauce
1 teaspoon finely minced seeded canned chipotle chilies*
1 teaspoon ground cumin
1 teaspoon sugar
⅔ cup chilled vodka

Ice cubes
6 celery stalks with leafy tops
6 fresh red chilies, slit

Mix first 7 ingredients in pitcher. Chill mixture until cold, at least 2 hours or overnight. Mix in vodka.

Fill 6 tall glasses with ice. Pour Bloody Mary mixture over. Garnish with celery stalks and chilies and serve.

*Chipotle *chilies canned in a spicy tomato sauce, sometimes called* adobo, *are available at Latin American markets, specialty foods stores and some supermarkets.*

6 SERVINGS

main courses

Opposite: Smoked Sausage Cassoulet (page 64). Left: Tuna, Tomato, Olive and Artichoke Sandwiches (page 85). Above: Pasta with Roasted Provençal Vegetable Sauce (page 108).

Beef Stew with Herbed Dumplings

Certain to be a favorite with your family, this hearty beef stew is flavored with bacon and paired with tender dumplings flecked with fresh chives and parsley.

STEW

- 4 pounds boneless beef chuck, cut into 1-inch cubes
- 2 tablespoons peanut oil

- 4 thick-sliced bacon strips, chopped
- 3 cups finely chopped onions
- 3 garlic cloves, finely chopped
- 1 teaspoon dried thyme
- 1 bay leaf
- 5½ cups canned beef broth
- 1 14½-ounce can crushed tomatoes with added puree

- 6 medium carrots, peeled, cut diagonally into 1-inch pieces
- 3 medium rutabagas, peeled, cut into ¾-inch pieces

DUMPLINGS

- ⅔ cup whole milk
- 2 large eggs
- 3 tablespoons minced fresh chives
- 2 tablespoons minced fresh Italian parsley

- 1½ cups unbleached all purpose flour
- 4 teaspoons baking powder
- ½ teaspoon salt

- 3 tablespoons cornstarch

FOR STEW: Position rack in center of oven; preheat to 325°F. Pat beef dry. Sprinkle with salt and pepper. Heat oil in heavy large ovenproof pot over medium-high heat. Working in batches, cook beef until brown, stirring occasionally and scraping up browned bits, about 8 minutes. Transfer meat to bowl.

Add bacon to same pot. Sauté until crisp, scraping up browned bits, about 5 minutes. Add onions, garlic, thyme and bay leaf. Cover and cook until onions are tender, stirring occasionally, about 10 minutes. Return beef and any accumulated juices to pot. Add 5 cups broth and tomatoes with puree. Cover; bring to simmer.

dinner in the kitchen for six

Confetti Salad with Ranch Dressing (page 139)

Beef Stew with Herbed Dumplings (opposite; pictured at left)

Guinness Stout or Beer

Pear and Maple Crumble (page 164)

Transfer pot to oven. Bake until beef is just tender, stirring occasionally, about 1 hour. Add carrots and rutabagas. Cover; bake until vegetables are crisp-tender, about 30 minutes. Uncover; bake until beef is very tender, about 25 minutes.

MEANWHILE, PREPARE DUMPLINGS: Whisk milk and eggs in medium bowl to blend. Stir in minced chives and parsley. Let milk mixture stand at room temperature 30 minutes.

Sift flour, baking powder and salt into large bowl. Add milk mixture. Stir just until blended.

Whisk remaining ½ cup canned beef broth and cornstarch in small bowl to blend. Bring stew to simmer over medium heat. Gradually stir cornstarch mixture into stew. Return stew to simmer, stirring until sauce thickens slightly.

Spoon dumpling batter in 12 dollops atop simmering stew. Cover tightly; simmer until dumplings are puffed and tester inserted into center of dumplings comes out clean, about 15 minutes.

Serve stew immediately with dumplings.

6 SERVINGS

romantic dinner
for two

Lobster Crisps in
Champagne-Dill Sauce (page 14)

Champagne

Beef Medallions with Cognac
Sauce (at right; pictured opposite)

Mashed Potatoes with
Pancetta and Leeks
(page 133; pictured opposite)

Sautéed Baby Vegetables

Cabernet Sauvignon

Chocolate-dipped Strawberries

Beef Medallions with Cognac Sauce

- 2 tablespoons (¼ stick) unsalted butter
- ¼ cup chopped shallots
- 1 teaspoon (packed) brown sugar
- 1 cup canned low salt chicken broth
- ½ cup canned beef broth
- ½ cup Cognac or brandy
- ¼ cup whipping cream

- 2 4- to 5-ounce beef tenderloin steaks (each about 1 inch thick)
- Chopped fresh chives

Melt 1 tablespoon butter in heavy medium saucepan over medium heat. Add shallots and sauté until tender, about 4 minutes. Add brown sugar; stir 1 minute. Add chicken broth, beef broth and Cognac. Simmer until sauce is reduced to ½ cup, about 20 minutes. Add cream. *(Can be made 1 day ahead. Cover; chill.)*

Sprinkle steaks with salt and pepper. Melt 1 tablespoon butter in heavy medium skillet over medium-high heat. Add steaks; cook to desired doneness, about 4 minutes per side for rare. Transfer steaks to plates. Add sauce to skillet; bring to boil, scraping up any browned bits. Season to taste with salt and pepper.

Slice steaks; fan on plates. Spoon sauce over. Garnish with chives.

2 SERVINGS

New York Steaks with Anchovy-Lemon Butter

- 2 tablespoons (¼ stick) unsalted butter, room temperature
- 9 canned anchovy fillets, minced
- 1 tablespoon minced shallot
- 1 teaspoon fresh lemon juice
- ½ teaspoon grated lemon peel
- 2 7-ounce New York strip steaks

Prepare barbecue (medium-high heat) or preheat broiler. Using fork, mash first 5 ingredients in bowl until blended. Chill. Sprinkle steaks with salt and pepper. Grill or broil to desired doneness, about 5 minutes per side for medium-rare. Transfer to plates. Top steaks with anchovy butter and serve.

2 SERVINGS

Rib-Eye Steaks with Béarnaise Butter

¼	cup dry white wine
1	tablespoon minced shallot
¼	teaspoon dried tarragon
5	tablespoons butter, room temperature
1	tablespoon minced fresh tarragon
	Olive oil
2	12-ounce rib-eye steaks (each about 1 to 1¼ inches thick)
	Dill Mashed Potatoes with Crème Fraîche and Caviar (recipe on page 125)

Boil wine, shallot and dried tarragon in small saucepan until liquid evaporates, about 2 minutes. Cool completely. Mix butter and fresh tarragon into shallot mixture. Season with salt and pepper. Form mixture into log; wrap in plastic; chill until firm. *(Can be made 3 days ahead. Keep chilled.)* Cut butter into ⅓-inch-thick slices. Bring to room temperature before continuing.

Brush large nonstick skillet with oil; heat over medium-high heat. Sprinkle steaks with salt and pepper; add to skillet. Cook to desired doneness, about 5 minutes per side for medium-rare. Overlap butter slices atop steaks and serve with mashed potatoes.

2 SERVINGS

it's in the sauce

Classic French cooking draws from a repertoire of hundreds of different sauces. Many of these have found their way into our everyday cooking and dining vernacular, as evidenced by the following familiar terms found in recipes and on many restaurant menus across the country:

- Béarnaise: Warm emulsion of egg yolks and melted butter seasoned with shallots, herbs, vinegar and white wine.
- Béchamel: White sauce consisting of milk thickened with roux, a cooked mixture of flour and butter.
- Beurre blanc: Warm, creamy sauce made by whisking cold butter into white wine vinegar reduced with chopped shallots.
- Crème anglaise: Literally "English cream"; a pourable, sweet custard sauce made with egg yolks, sugar, vanilla and milk or cream.
- Hollandaise: Warm emulsion of egg yolks and butter, usually seasoned with lemon juice and a touch of nutmeg.
- Mayonnaise: Cold emulsion of egg yolks and olive oil, often seasoned with lemon juice or vinegar and mustard.
- Mornay: A béchamel enriched with grated Parmesan and Gruyère cheeses.
- Velouté: Chicken, veal or fish stock thickened with a flour and butter roux.

Grilled Mustard-Dill Burgers

- 3 tablespoons sour cream
- 3 tablespoons Dijon mustard
- 1½ tablespoons chopped fresh dill
- 10 ounces lean ground beef

- 2 hamburger buns, split
- 2 tomato slices
- 2 Bibb lettuce leaves

Prepare barbecue (medium-high heat). Mix first 3 ingredients in medium bowl. Transfer 3 tablespoons sauce to small bowl and reserve. Add meat to remaining sauce in medium bowl and mix gently to blend. Divide meat mixture into 2 equal portions. Flatten each to ½-inch-thick patty; sprinkle with salt and pepper.

Grill cut side of buns until toasted, about 1 minute. Grill patties to desired doneness, about 4 minutes per side for medium. Spread bottom half of buns with reserved sauce. Top each with burger, tomato slice, lettuce and bun top.

2 SERVINGS

easy lunch for two

Grilled Mustard-Dill Burgers (at left; pictured at left)

Potato Chips

Dill Pickles

Macaroni Salad

Corn on the Cob

Lemonade

Chocolate Chunk and Pecan Cookies (page 209)

Barbecued Texas Beef Brisket

DRY RUB

½ cup paprika
3 tablespoons ground black pepper
3 tablespoons coarse salt
3 tablespoons sugar
2 tablespoons chili powder
1 7½- to 8-pound untrimmed whole beef brisket

MOP

12 ounces beer
½ cup cider vinegar
½ cup water
¼ cup vegetable oil
2 tablespoons Worcestershire sauce
2 tablespoons minced jalapeño chilies
5 pounds (about) 100% natural lump charcoal
4 cups (about) oak wood smoke chips, soaked in water 30 minutes
1 cup purchased barbecue sauce (such as Bull's-Eye)
1 tablespoon chili powder

FOR DRY RUB: Mix first 5 ingredients in small bowl. Transfer 1 tablespoon dry rub to another small bowl; reserve for mop. Spread remaining dry rub all over brisket. Cover; chill overnight.

FOR MOP: Mix first 6 ingredients plus reserved rub in heavy medium saucepan. Stir over low heat 5 minutes. Pour ½ cup mop into bowl. Cover; chill for use in sauce. Cover and chill remaining mop.

Following manufacturer's instructions and using natural lump charcoal, start fire in smoker. When charcoal is ash-gray, drain ½ cup wood chips and scatter over charcoal. Bring smoker to 200°F to 225°F, regulating temperature by opening vents wider to increase temperature and closing slightly to reduce temperature.

Place brisket, fat side up, on rack in smoker. Cover; cook until tender when pierced with fork and meat thermometer inserted into center registers 185°F, about 10 hours (turn brisket over for last 30 minutes). Every 1½ to 2 hours, add enough charcoal to maintain single layer and to maintain 200°F to 225°F temperature; add ½ cup drained wood chips. Brush brisket with chilled mop in pan each time smoker is opened. Transfer brisket to platter; let stand 15 minutes.

Combine barbecue sauce and chili powder in saucepan. Add any juices from brisket; bring to boil, thinning with some of reserved ½ cup mop, if desired. Thinly slice brisket; serve with sauce.

12 SERVINGS

back-yard barbecue for twelve

Chips and Dip

Barbecued Texas Beef Brisket (at right; pictured opposite)

Mixed Greens, Tomato and Red Onion Salad

Corn on the Cob

Potato Salad

Beer, Iced Tea and Sodas

Vanilla Ice Cream

Ginger-Molasses Cookies (page 193)

Beef Barley Soup with Wild Mushrooms and Parsnips

A mix of wild mushrooms, along with parsnips, bell peppers and carrots, adds great flavor to this warming cold-weather soup. Make it two days ahead, if you like.

- 3 tablespoons olive oil
- 1½ pounds assorted fresh wild mushrooms (such as crimini and oyster), sliced
- ¾ pound onions, chopped
- 2 celery stalks, chopped
- 4 large garlic cloves, chopped
- 3½ pounds center-cut beef shank slices (about ¾ to 1 inch thick)
- 8 cups canned beef broth
- 7 cups water
- 1¼ pounds red bell peppers, chopped
- 1 pound parsnips, peeled, cut into ½-inch pieces
- ½ pound carrots, peeled, cut into ½-inch pieces
- 1¾ cups pearl barley (about 9 ounces)
- 1½ cups canned crushed tomatoes with added puree
- 2 ¾-ounce packages dried porcini mushrooms,* brushed clean of any grit, coarsely chopped
- 2 tablespoons dried marjoram
- 1 tablespoon dried thyme

Heat oil in heavy large pot over medium-high heat. Add mushrooms and onions. Sauté until mushrooms brown, about 18 minutes. Add celery and garlic and stir 1 minute. Add beef shank slices and all remaining ingredients. Bring to boil. Reduce heat to medium-low. Cover and simmer until meat is tender, about 1½ hours. Remove soup from heat.

Using tongs, remove meat from pot. Cool slightly. Remove meat from bones; discard bones and any tough connective tissue. Cut meat into bite-size pieces and return to soup. Season soup to taste with salt and pepper. *(Can be made 2 days ahead. Cool slightly at room temperature. Chill uncovered until cold, then cover and keep chilled. Rewarm soup over medium heat.)*

**Porcini mushrooms are available at Italian markets, specialty foods stores and many supermarkets.*

8 SERVINGS

Veal Scaloppine with
Spring Pea Coulis and Asparagus
(at right; pictured at right)

Thyme-roasted Potatoes with
Balsamic Vinegar
(page 125; pictured at right)

Chardonnay

Strawberry and Champagne Ice
(page 184)

Veal Scaloppine with Spring Pea Coulis and Asparagus

1¼ pounds slender asparagus spears, trimmed

Nonstick vegetable oil spray
¼ cup finely chopped shallots
2 cups frozen petite peas (about 9 ounces), thawed
¾ cup canned low-salt chicken broth
3 teaspoons minced fresh tarragon

6 3-ounce boneless veal round cutlets, each cut into 3 pieces

Cook asparagus in large pot of boiling salted water until crisp-tender, about 3 minutes. Drain. Place asparagus in large bowl of ice water to cool. Drain; pat dry.

Spray medium nonstick skillet with nonstick spray. Heat skillet over medium heat. Add shallots and sauté 1 minute. Add peas and sauté 2 minutes. Add broth. Bring to simmer. Transfer mixture to blender. Add 1 teaspoon tarragon. Puree until smooth, about 3 minutes. Season pea coulis with salt and pepper.

Pound each veal piece between sheets of plastic wrap to scant ¼-inch thickness. *(Can be made 1 day ahead. Wrap asparagus in paper towels. Cover asparagus, pea coulis and veal separately; chill.)*

Spray 2 large nonstick skillets with nonstick spray. Heat over medium-high heat. Sprinkle veal with salt and pepper. Working in batches, add veal to skillets; sauté until brown and just cooked through, about 2 minutes per side. Transfer to platter. Tent with foil.

Divide asparagus and remaining 2 teaspoons tarragon between same 2 skillets. Sauté over medium-high heat until asparagus is heated through, about 2 minutes. Rewarm coulis in heavy small saucepan over medium-low heat.

Spoon 3 tablespoons pea coulis onto each of 6 plates. Place veal atop coulis. Arrange asparagus alongside veal.

6 SERVINGS

Veal Chops with Arugula Salad

- 6 tablespoons olive oil (preferably extra-virgin)
- 1 tablespoon balsamic vinegar

- 4 6- to 8-ounce veal loin chops (each about ¾ inch thick)
- 4 teaspoons ground sage

- 4 cups (packed) arugula leaves (about 4 large bunches)
- ⅓ cup chopped red onion

The loin chops are pounded until thin so that they cook quickly, then topped with a colorful salad of arugula and red onion.

Whisk 3 tablespoons oil and vinegar in large bowl. Season to taste with salt and pepper; set dressing aside.

Place chops between 2 large pieces of plastic wrap on work surface, spacing apart. Using meat mallet, pound veal surrounding bone to ½-inch thickness. Rub each side of each chop with ½ teaspoon sage. Sprinkle with salt and pepper.

Heat remaining 3 tablespoons oil in heavy large skillet over medium-high heat. Add chops; cook about 3 minutes per side for medium-rare. Transfer to platter; cover and keep warm.

Whisk any drippings from skillet into dressing. Add arugula and onion to dressing; toss to coat. Top chops with arugula salad.

4 SERVINGS

Broiled Veal Chops with Mixed Peppercorns

dinner by the fire for six

Broiled Veal Chops with Mixed Peppercorns (at right; pictured opposite)

Broccoli Rabe with Garlic and Pecorino Romano Cheese (page 132; pictured opposite)

Roasted New Potatoes

Cranberry-Apple Crisp (page 166)

- 6 ¾-inch-thick veal loin chops (about 6 to 8 ounces each), trimmed
- 3 tablespoons olive oil
- 2 tablespoons coarsely ground mixed peppercorns
- 1 tablespoon minced fresh rosemary

Place veal chops in baking dish. Brush with oil, then sprinkle both sides with peppercorns and rosemary. Let stand 1 hour.

Preheat broiler. Transfer veal chops to broiler pan. Sprinkle with salt. Broil veal 6 inches from heat source to desired doneness, about 5 minutes per side for medium-rare. Transfer veal to plates. Pour any accumulated broiler pan drippings over veal and serve.

6 SERVINGS

Veal with Mushrooms and Tomatoes

- 4 tablespoons olive oil
- 2 large garlic cloves, chopped
- ¾ teaspoon chopped fresh rosemary
- 12 ounces mushrooms, sliced
- 12 ounces plum tomatoes, seeded, chopped
- 1 pound thin veal cutlets
- All purpose flour
- 1 cup canned low-salt chicken broth
- ½ cup dry white wine

Heat 2 tablespoons oil in heavy large saucepan over medium-high heat. Add garlic and rosemary; stir 30 seconds. Add mushrooms. Cover pan and cook 5 minutes, stirring occasionally. Uncover and sauté until mushrooms are golden brown, about 5 minutes longer. Add tomatoes and cook until softened, about 5 minutes. Set aside.

Sprinkle veal with salt and pepper. Dust with flour. Heat 1 tablespoon oil in heavy large skillet over medium-high heat. Add half of veal. Sauté until cooked through, 2 minutes per side. Transfer to platter; tent with foil. Repeat with remaining oil and veal.

Add broth and wine to same skillet. Boil until reduced by half, scraping up browned bits, about 4 minutes. Add mushroom mixture and stir to blend. Season with salt and pepper; spoon over veal.

4 SERVINGS

Lamb Chops with Asian Pear and Kiwi Salsa

- 2 small Asian pears, cored, diced
- 3 large kiwis, peeled, diced
- 6 tablespoons dried cranberries
- ¼ cup chopped green onions
- 2 tablespoons fresh lemon juice
- 3 tablespoons honey
- 3 tablespoons chopped fresh mint

- 8 1-inch-thick lamb rib chops

Combine pears, kiwis, cranberries, onions and lemon juice in medium bowl; mix in 2 tablespoons honey and 2 tablespoons chopped mint. Season salsa to taste with salt and pepper. Let stand 30 minutes, tossing occasionally.

Preheat broiler. Brush chops lightly on both sides with remaining 1 tablespoon honey; sprinkle with salt, pepper and remaining 1 tablespoon chopped fresh mint. Broil chops until cooked to desired doneness, about 5 minutes per side for medium-rare.

Transfer 2 lamb chops to each plate. Spoon salsa alongside.

4 SERVINGS

fusion dinner for four

Lamb Chops with Asian Pear and Kiwi Salsa (at right; pictured at right)

Sautéed String Beans

Rice Pilaf

Petite Syrah

Ginger and Vanilla Bean Crème Brûlée (page 180)

Lamb Shanks with Potatoes, Parsnips and Olives

6 12- to 16-ounce lamb shanks
3 tablespoons olive oil

4 medium carrots, peeled, cut into ¼-inch-thick rounds
2½ cups chopped onions
1½ cups sliced celery
2 garlic cloves, minced
2 teaspoons dried rosemary
2 teaspoons dried oregano
1 28-ounce can diced tomatoes in juice
2 cups water
2 cups dry red wine
1 3 x 1-inch piece orange peel (orange part only)

12 baby red-skinned potatoes
6 medium carrots, peeled, cut into 2-inch pieces
6 medium parsnips, peeled, cut into 2-inch pieces
½ cup Kalamata olives, pitted

Sprinkle lamb with salt and pepper. Heat 3 tablespoons oil in heavy large pot over medium-high heat. Working in batches, cook lamb until brown, about 8 minutes. Transfer to large bowl.

Reduce heat to medium. Add carrot rounds, onions and celery to pot. Sauté until vegetables are tender and golden, about 10 minutes. Add garlic, rosemary and oregano. Sauté 1 minute. Stir in tomatoes with juices, 2 cups water, wine and orange peel. Return lamb to pot, pressing to submerge. Bring to boil. Reduce heat to low. Cover; simmer until lamb is just tender, about 2 hours 15 minutes.

Add potatoes, 2-inch carrot pieces, parsnips and olives to pot. Simmer uncovered until vegetables are tender and lamb is very tender, about 30 minutes. Using slotted spoon, transfer lamb and vegetables to platter. Boil juices in pot until thickened enough to coat spoon, 5 minutes. Discard orange peel. Season sauce with salt and pepper.

Spoon sauce over lamb and vegetables and serve.

6 SERVINGS

humble cuts

Time was, cuts of meat that were anything less than the tenderest or most meaty were considered "humble." Tough, bony or gristly, they were consigned to bargain sale or reserved for the butchers' own use or for a kitchen crew's meals.

Of course, butchers and chefs knew something most of the public didn't: These humble cuts have rich flavor and a texture that can be coaxed to full glory through slow, gentle cooking. Look for these cuts:

- Breast (lamb): A rib section sold with or without bones that is good braised.
- Brisket (beef): Located just behind the shank, this boneless cut is best braised.
- Chuck (beef): A tough shoulder cut that can be either braised or stewed.
- Neck (lamb): Sold as bone-in slices, neck meat is good in stews.
- Shank (beef, lamb): Lamb shank is left whole; beef shank is cut crosswise into sections or boned and cubed. Both lend themselves to braising or stewing.
- Short ribs (beef): Cut from between the neck and shoulder blade, these are good for stewing.
- Shoulder (lamb, pork): Cubed shoulder can be used for kebabs or stews.

Lamb Stew with Spinach and Garbanzo Beans

This comforting dish is easy to make with canned garbanzo beans and ready-to-use packaged spinach leaves. Serve the stew over steamed white rice, if you like, to soak up all of the delicious juices.

- 1¼ pounds lamb shoulder or stew meat, cut into 1-inch pieces
- Garlic powder
- 3 tablespoons olive oil
- 1 onion, coarsely chopped
- 1 cup ½-inch pieces peeled carrots
- 1 15-ounce can garbanzo beans (chickpeas), drained
- ½ cup canned chicken broth
- ½ cup tomato sauce
- 1 tablespoon fresh lemon juice

- 1 10-ounce package ready-to-use spinach leaves
- Lemon wedges

Sprinkle lamb with salt, pepper and garlic powder. Heat oil in heavy large pot over medium-high heat. Add lamb and sauté until brown, about 10 minutes. Add onion and carrots and sauté until beginning to brown, about 5 minutes. Add garbanzo beans, broth, tomato sauce and lemon juice; bring to simmer. Reduce heat to medium-low, cover pot and simmer until lamb is tender, about 1 hour.

Add spinach to stew. Cover and cook until spinach wilts, stirring, 8 minutes. Season with salt and pepper. Serve with lemon.

4 SERVINGS

Rack of Lamb with Spice-and-Pepper Crust

- 1 1¼- to 1½-pound rack of lamb, trimmed
- 1 teaspoon cumin seeds
- 1 teaspoon coriander seeds
- 1 teaspoon green peppercorns
- 2 large garlic cloves, chopped
- 1 tablespoon grated orange peel
- 1 tablespoon extra-virgin olive oil

Preheat oven to 450°F. Sprinkle lamb with salt and pepper. Enclose cumin seeds, coriander seeds and green peppercorns in small resealable plastic bag. Using mallet, coarsely crush seeds and peppercorns. Add chopped garlic cloves, grated orange peel and extra-virgin olive oil to bag and mash to coarse paste. Smear spice paste over meat portion of rack of lamb.

Place lamb, paste side up, in small baking pan. Roast lamb 10 minutes. Reduce oven temperature to 400°F. Continue to roast until thermometer inserted into lamb registers 135°F for medium-rare, approximately 15 minutes longer. Cut lamb between bones into chops and then serve immediately.

2 SERVINGS

sophisticated dinner for two

Rack of Lamb with Spice-and-Pepper Crust (opposite; pictured at left)

Potato Gratin

Purchased Caponata

Merlot

Lemon Tartlets from the Bakery

Grilled Lamb Chops with Lemon and Thyme

½ cup Dijon mustard
½ cup fresh lemon juice
6 tablespoons balsamic vinegar
3 tablespoons chopped fresh thyme
1 teaspoon ground black pepper
⅔ cup extra-virgin olive oil
24 lamb rib chops or loin chops

1 lemon, halved
Fresh thyme sprigs (optional)
Lemon wedges (optional)

Mix mustard, lemon juice, vinegar, chopped thyme and pepper in medium bowl. Gradually whisk in oil. Divide marinade between 2 large shallow glass baking dishes. Add 12 chops to each dish; turn to coat in marinade. Cover with plastic and refrigerate at least 2 hours and up to 4 hours.

Prepare barbecue (medium-high heat) or preheat broiler. Grill or broil lamb to desired doneness, about 7 minutes per side for medium-rare. Transfer lamb chops to platter. Season with salt. Squeeze juice from lemon halves over chops. Garnish platter with fresh thyme sprigs and lemon wedges, if desired.

8 SERVINGS

wine-tasting party for eight

Assorted Chiantis

Cheese Platter

Mushroom and Red Bell Pepper Salad

Grilled Lamb Chops with Lemon and Thyme (at right; pictured at right)

Roasted Red Potatoes and Red Onions

Green Beans with Pesto

Flourless Chocolate Cake with Chocolate Glaze (page 168)

Grappa and Espresso

Roast Leg of Lamb with Potatoes and Onions

Garlic, rosemary and thyme, along with roasted potatoes and onions, lend a Provençal flavor to roast leg of lamb.

- 1 6- to 7-pound bone-in leg of lamb, excess fat trimmed
- 3 large garlic cloves, thinly sliced
- 1 tablespoon extra-virgin olive oil
- 1 tablespoon minced fresh thyme or 1½ teaspoons dried
- 2 teaspoons minced fresh savory or 1 teaspoon dried
- 1 teaspoon minced fresh rosemary or ¾ teaspoon dried
- 1 teaspoon salt
- ¾ teaspoon ground black pepper

- 3½ pounds russet potatoes, unpeeled, cut into ¼-inch-thick rounds
- 2½ pounds onions, thinly sliced (about 8 cups)
- 1¾ cups beef stock or canned beef broth

Preheat oven to 400°F. Using small sharp knife, cut 1-inch-deep, ½-inch-long slits all over lamb. Insert garlic slices into slits. Rub oil all over lamb. Mix thyme, savory, rosemary, salt and pepper in small bowl. Rub herb mixture all over lamb. Set aside.

Generously butter large roasting pan. Combine potatoes, onions and stock in large pot (stock will not cover vegetables). Bring to boil. Reduce heat, cover and simmer until potatoes are halfway tender, about 10 minutes. Transfer potato mixture to prepared pan; spread evenly in pan. Sprinkle with salt and pepper. Bake 10 minutes. Reduce oven temperature to 375°F.

Place lamb in roasting pan atop potato mixture. Roast until thermometer inserted into thickest part of lamb registers 130°F for medium-rare, about 1 hour 50 minutes. Remove from oven. Tent with foil and let stand 15 minutes.

Thinly slice lamb. Arrange lamb on large platter. Surround with potato mixture and any juices from pan and serve.

6 TO 8 SERVINGS

lunch buffet for ten

Grilled Lamb Sandwiches with Grilled Green Onions
(at right; pictured at right)

Roasted Potato Salad with Sage
(page 136; pictured at right)

Artichoke, Lima and Pea Salad
(page 141; pictured at right)

Sodas and Bottled Water

Lemon Curd Layer Cake
(page 172)

Grilled Lamb Sandwiches with Grilled Green Onions

- 1 4½-pound butterflied boned leg of lamb, trimmed of excess fat
- 6 garlic cloves, thinly sliced
- 2 tablespoons minced fresh thyme
- 1 tablespoon dried savory
- 1 tablespoon minced fresh rosemary

- 5 bunches green onions, trimmed
- ¼ cup plus 3 tablespoons extra-virgin olive oil
- 2 French-bread baguettes, each cut crosswise into five 4- to 4½-inch pieces

- Garlic Mayonnaise (see recipe opposite)
- Red Bell Pepper Sauce (see recipe opposite)
- 1½ cups purchased tapenade*

Using sharp knife, cut ½-inch slits all over lamb. Insert garlic slices into slits. Sprinkle lamb with salt and pepper, then herbs, pressing herbs to adhere. *(Can be prepared 1 day ahead. Cover and chill.)*

Prepare barbecue (medium-high heat). Place green onions in large roasting pan. Drizzle ¼ cup oil over onions; toss to coat. Sprinkle with salt and pepper. Cut baguette pieces horizontally in half. Brush cut sides of bread with remaining 3 tablespoons oil.

Grill lamb until meat thermometer inserted into thickest part registers 135°F for medium-rare, turning occasionally, about 30 minutes. Transfer to platter and tent with foil. Let stand 10 minutes.

Working in batches, arrange onions in single layer on grill. Grill until beginning to brown, about 4 minutes per side. Transfer to cutting board. Grill baguettes, cut side down, until golden, 2 minutes.

Chop onions. Place in bowl. Cut lamb diagonally into thin slices and arrange on platter. Serve lamb with onions, baguettes, mayonnaise, bell pepper sauce and tapenade.

*Tapenade *is a thick olive paste or spread available at Italian markets and also at some supermarkets.*

10 SERVINGS

These are great for a big group because the guests can assemble the sandwiches themselves, piling on rosy slices of lamb, chopped grilled green onions and a variety of condiments, including two easy spreads—a garlic mayonnaise, and a sauce of mayonnaise and roasted red peppers.

Garlic Mayonnaise

- 6 garlic cloves
- ⅓ cup extra-virgin olive oil
- 2 cups purchased mayonnaise

Finely chop garlic cloves in food processor. Gradually blend in oil. Add mayonnaise. Blend until smooth. Season with salt and pepper. *(Can be made 1 day ahead. Cover and chill.)*

MAKES ABOUT 2⅓ CUPS

Red Bell Pepper Sauce

- 1 15-ounce jar roasted red bell peppers, well drained, patted dry
- 1 cup Garlic Mayonnaise (see recipe above)

Blend roasted peppers and 1 cup mayonnaise in processor until mixture is smooth. Season to taste with salt and pepper. Transfer sauce to small bowl. *(Can be made 1 day ahead. Cover; chill.)*

MAKES ABOUT 2 CUPS

Kansas City Spareribs

¾ cup (packed) golden brown sugar
½ cup paprika
2½ tablespoons coarse salt
2½ tablespoons ground black pepper
1 tablespoon onion powder
½ teaspoon cayenne pepper
3 large racks spareribs (about 9 pounds)

8 pounds (about) 100% natural lump charcoal or charcoal briquettes
4 cups (about) oak or hickory wood smoke chips, soaked in cold water at least 30 minutes

1½ cups purchased tomato-based barbecue sauce (such as KC Masterpiece)

Mix brown sugar, paprika, coarse salt, black pepper, onion powder and cayenne pepper in small bowl for dry rub. Sprinkle ⅔ cup dry rub all over spareribs. Cover ribs with plastic wrap; refrigerate overnight. Cover remaining dry rub; store at room temperature.

Unwrap seasoned spareribs; sprinkle all over with half of remaining dry rub. Let stand at room temperature 30 minutes.

Following manufacturer's instructions and using natural lump charcoal and ½ cup drained wood chips for smoker, start fire and bring temperature of smoker to 200°F to 225°F. Arrange ribs on rack in smoker. Cover and cook ribs 2 hours, turning occasionally. Add more charcoal as needed to maintain temperature and more drained wood chips (½ cup with each addition) to maintain smoke level.

Sprinkle ribs evenly with all remaining dry rub. Cover and cook 1 hour 15 minutes. Brush ribs generously with barbecue sauce. Continue cooking until meat is very tender and brown, about 30 minutes longer. Maintain temperature by adding more charcoal; maintain smoke level by adding more drained wood chips as needed.

Transfer ribs to large serving platter. Let stand 10 minutes. Cut rib racks between bones into individual ribs and serve immediately.

8 SERVINGS

pool party for eight

Kansas City Spareribs (at right; pictured opposite)

Hot and Smoky Baked Beans (page 124)

Coleslaw

Chipotle Corn Bread (page 151)

Iced Tea

S'mores Sundaes (page 189)

Smoked Sausage Cassoulet

one-dish supper for eight

Crudités with
Purchased Goat Cheese Dip

Smoked Sausage Cassoulet
(at right; pictured on page 38)

Fougasse with Provençal Herbs
(page 150)

Red Wine

Coffee Ice Cream

Twice-baked Almond Cookies
(page 194)

- 2 tablespoons plus ¼ cup olive oil
- 3 pounds assorted fully cooked smoked sausages (such as kielbasa and andouille)

- 4 large leeks (white and pale green parts only), thinly sliced
- 6 large garlic cloves, chopped
- 1 medium apple, peeled, chopped
- 1 tablespoon chopped fresh rosemary
- 1½ teaspoons dried rubbed sage
- ½ cup brandy
- 2 14½-ounce cans diced tomatoes with roasted garlic in juice
- 3 15-ounce cans Great Northern beans, drained, liquid reserved
- 1 10-ounce package frozen baby lima beans, thawed
- 1 cup (or more) canned chicken broth
- 3 tablespoons tomato paste
- ½ teaspoon ground cloves

- 4 cups diced country-style bread
- 1 pound tomatoes, seeded, diced
- ½ cup chopped fresh parsley

Preheat oven to 350°F. Heat 2 tablespoons oil in heavy large ovenproof pot over medium heat. Add sausages; sauté until brown, about 25 minutes. Transfer to plate and cut into ½-inch rounds.

Add leeks and garlic to same pot. Sauté until beginning to soften, about 8 minutes. Mix in apple, rosemary and sage. Add brandy and simmer until almost evaporated, about 5 minutes. Mix in canned tomatoes with juices, canned beans with ½ cup reserved liquid, lima beans, 1 cup broth, tomato paste and cloves. Add sausages. Season cassoulet with pepper.

Bring cassoulet to boil. Cover pot and transfer to preheated oven; bake 30 minutes. *(Can be made up to 2 days ahead. Uncover; cool 1 hour. Refrigerate until cold; then cover and keep refrigerated. Before continuing, rewarm in covered pot in 350°F oven 40 minutes, adding more chicken broth if dry.)*

Heat remaining ¼ cup oil in heavy large skillet over medium heat. Add bread and sauté until golden brown, stirring often, about 25 minutes. Combine fresh tomatoes and parsley in large bowl; mix in bread. Season topping with salt and pepper. Spoon onto warm cassoulet. Bake uncovered 15 minutes longer and serve.

8 TO 10 SERVINGS

Basil mayonnaise and avocado slices add an extra dimension to the good old bacon, lettuce and tomato sandwich. To get a head start, make the mayonnaise a day ahead.

The Best BLTs

- 2½ cups (lightly packed) fresh basil leaves
- 1 cup mayonnaise
- ¼ cup (½ stick) butter, room temperature

- 12 thick-sliced bacon strips (about 1 pound)

- 12 ½-inch-thick slices fresh country-style white bread
- 3 large tomatoes, cut into ¼-inch-thick rounds
- 2 ripe avocados, pitted, peeled, sliced
- 1 red onion, thinly sliced
- 6 lettuce leaves

Mix basil, mayonnaise and butter in processor until basil is finely chopped and mixture is well blended. Season to taste with salt and pepper. *(Can be made 1 day ahead. Cover and refrigerate.)*

Cook bacon in heavy large skillet over medium-high heat until crisp, about 8 minutes. Transfer to paper towels; drain.

Spread half of mayonnaise mixture over 1 side of 6 bread slices. Top each with 2 tomato slices. Sprinkle tomatoes with salt and pepper. Top tomato slices with avocado, then with bacon strips, onion and lettuce. Spread remaining mayonnaise mixture over remaining 6 bread slices. Place slices atop lettuce. Cut sandwiches in half; serve.

6 SERVINGS

Roast Chicken with Rosemary-Orange Butter

sunday supper
for four

Carrot Soup with
Thyme and Fennel
(page 30; pictured opposite)

Roast Chicken with
Rosemary-Orange Butter
(at right; pictured opposite)

Roasted Potatoes

Sautéed Swiss Chard
(page 128)

Pinot Noir or Sauvignon Blanc

Pear and Fig Pie
(page 154)

- 3 shallots
- 6 tablespoons (¾ stick) butter, room temperature
- 4 teaspoons minced fresh rosemary
- 1 tablespoon grated orange peel

- 1 7-pound whole roasting chicken, neck and heart reserved

- 1 medium onion, chopped
- 2 medium carrots, peeled, chopped
- 1 celery stalk, chopped

- ¾ cup dry white wine
- 1½ cups canned low-salt chicken broth

Position rack in center of oven; preheat to 400°F. Mince 1 shallot; mix with butter, rosemary and peel in small bowl. Season with salt and pepper. Set rosemary-orange butter aside.

Pat chicken dry. Using fingers, loosen skin from chicken breasts, legs and thighs. Sprinkle chicken cavity with salt and pepper. Spread half of rosemary-orange butter under chicken skin. Tie chicken legs together to hold shape. Spread remaining butter over chicken. Sprinkle chicken with salt and pepper.

Place rack in large roasting pan. Add reserved chicken neck and heart to pan, then onion, carrots and celery. Chop remaining 2 shallots; add to pan. Place chicken, breast side up, on rack in pan. Roast chicken until meat thermometer inserted into innermost part of thigh registers 180°F, stirring vegetables in pan occasionally, about 1 hour 40 minutes. Transfer chicken to platter. Tent with foil while making sauce (do not clean pan).

Place same roasting pan over medium-high heat. Add wine to pan; simmer until most of wine evaporates, scraping up any browned bits, about 5 minutes. Add broth. Simmer until sauce is reduced to 1½ cups, stirring often, about 6 minutes. Strain into 2-cup glass measuring cup; discard solids. Spoon fat from top of sauce. Season to taste with salt and pepper. Serve chicken with pan sauce.

4 SERVINGS

Curried Chicken

This chicken curry goes well with steamed white rice and a variety of condiments, from the yogurt and chopped cucumber mixture called *raita* to shredded coconut. If you like, stop by an Indian restaurant and pick up some *naan,* a tender flatbread, to mop up the flavorful curry sauce.

- 3 tablespoons vegetable oil
- 3 cups chopped onions
- ¼ cup minced peeled fresh ginger
- 3 garlic cloves, minced
- 3 tablespoons curry powder
- 1 teaspoon ground cumin
- ¼ teaspoon ground cinnamon
- 2 tablespoons all purpose flour
- 1 cup plain yogurt
- 3 tablespoons tomato paste
- 3 cups canned low-salt chicken broth
- 1 cup unsweetened applesauce

- 4 pounds skinless boneless chicken breasts, cut crosswise into ½-inch-thick slices
- 1 10-ounce package frozen peas
- ½ cup sour cream
- ½ cup canned unsweetened coconut milk*
- Fresh cilantro sprigs

Steamed white rice, Major Grey mango chutney, sliced peeled bananas, chopped pitted peeled mangoes, shredded unsweetened coconut, chopped toasted peanuts

Heat oil in heavy large pot over medium heat. Add onions and sauté until golden, 15 minutes. Add ginger and garlic; sauté 1 minute. Add curry, cumin and cinnamon; sauté 1 minute. Add flour, then yogurt and tomato paste, whisking until sauce is smooth, 1 minute. Add broth and applesauce. Bring to boil. Reduce heat; simmer until sauce thickens slightly, stirring occasionally, 30 minutes. *(Can be made 1 day ahead. Cool slightly. Cover; chill. Return to simmer.)*

Add chicken and peas to sauce. Simmer until chicken is almost cooked through, 3 minutes. Add sour cream and coconut milk. Reduce heat to medium-low. Stir until chicken is cooked through and sauce thickens enough to coat spoon, 3 minutes (do not boil). Season with salt and pepper. Transfer to bowl. Garnish with cilantro.

Place rice, chutney, bananas, mangoes, coconut and peanuts in separate bowls. Serve alongside curry.

**Available at Indian, Southeast Asian and Latin American markets and at many supermarkets nationwide.*

8 TO 10 SERVINGS

Spicy Grilled Chicken and Green Onions

- 2 tablespoons vegetable oil
- 1 tablespoon hot pepper sauce
- 2 teaspoons honey
- 1 teaspoon paprika
- 7 green onions
- 2 skinless boneless chicken breast halves

Prepare barbecue (medium-high heat). Whisk oil, hot sauce, honey and paprika in 9-inch glass pie dish to blend. Mince 1 green onion; mix into marinade. Transfer 2 tablespoons marinade to small bowl and reserve. Add chicken to marinade in pie dish and turn to coat. Let stand 10 minutes, turning occasionally.

Sprinkle chicken and remaining whole green onions with salt. Grill chicken and whole onions until chicken is cooked through and onions soften, turning occasionally, about 10 minutes. Transfer chicken and onions to plates. Drizzle with reserved 2 tablespoons marinade and serve immediately.

2 SERVINGS

quick midweek dinner for two

Citrus Cooler
(page 33)

Spicy Grilled Chicken and Green Onions
(at left; pictured at left)

Deli Potato Salad

Dark Chocolate Brownies with White Chocolate Chunks
(page 192)

Chicken with Mustard Cream on Watercress

- 1 bunch watercress, stems trimmed
- 2 skinless boneless chicken breast halves

- 1 tablespoon butter
- ⅓ cup canned low-salt chicken broth
- ¼ cup whipping cream
- 2½ tablespoons honey Dijon mustard

Divide watercress between 2 plates. Place chicken between sheets of waxed paper. Using rolling pin, pound chicken to ½-inch thickness. Peel off paper. Sprinkle chicken with salt and pepper.

Melt butter in heavy medium skillet over medium heat. Add chicken; sauté until cooked through, about 4 minutes per side. Place chicken atop watercress. Add broth, cream and mustard to skillet. Boil until sauce thickens, whisking often, about 2 minutes. Season with salt and pepper. Spoon sauce over chicken.

2 SERVINGS

alfresco dinner for two

Chicken with Mustard Cream on Watercress
(at right; pictured at right)

Couscous with Red Bell Pepper, Carrots and Dill

French Bread

Chenin Blanc

Fresh Raspberries Drizzled with Framboise

Southwestern Chicken Chili

6 large chicken breast halves with skin and bones

3 tablespoons vegetable oil
3 large onions, coarsely chopped
6 garlic cloves, minced
1 jalapeño chili, minced
¼ cup chili powder
3 tablespoons ground cumin
1 tablespoon dried oregano
2 teaspoons ground coriander
1 28-ounce can crushed tomatoes in puree
2 12-ounce bottles of beer
2½ cups canned low-salt chicken broth

2 15¼-ounce cans kidney beans, rinsed, drained

Salsa, crushed tortilla chips, chopped green onions, sour cream and grated cheddar cheese

Here's a satisfying main course prepared with chicken instead of the typical beef. Jalapeño and cumin give it southwestern flavor. Serve the chili with your favorite condiments.

Arrange chicken in single layer in large skillet. Add enough water to cover chicken; bring to boil. Reduce heat, cover and simmer gently until chicken is cooked through, about 12 minutes. Drain chicken; cool slightly. Remove skin and bones; coarsely shred meat. *(Can be made 1 day ahead. Cover and refrigerate.)*

Heat oil in heavy large pot over medium-high heat. Add onions and sauté until tender, about 10 minutes. Add garlic and jalapeño chili; sauté 1 minute. Mix in chili powder, cumin, oregano and coriander. Add tomatoes, beer and broth. Simmer over medium-low heat 1 hour to blend flavors, stirring occasionally.

Add beans to chili. Simmer uncovered until chili thickens, stirring occasionally, about 30 minutes. Add shredded chicken. Simmer chili until chicken is heated through.

Ladle chili into bowls. Serve with bowls of salsa, tortilla chips, green onions, sour cream and cheddar cheese.

10 TO 12 SERVINGS

Chicken and Vegetable Pot Pie

homestyle supper for eight

Tossed Salad with Blue Cheese Dressing

Chicken and Vegetable Pot Pie (at right; pictured opposite)

Sautéed String Beans

Chardonnay

Baked Apples

❖

4 pounds chicken breasts with skin and bones
4 to 6 cups canned low-salt chicken broth

3 large carrots, peeled, cut into ½-inch pieces
1 pound turnips, peeled, cut into ½-inch pieces
1 large bunch turnip greens (about 8 to 10 ounces), center stem cut away, leaves cut into 1-inch pieces

¼ cup (½ stick) butter
3 medium leeks (white and pale green parts only), sliced
2 large shallots, minced
2 tablespoons minced fresh thyme
½ cup all purpose flour
½ cup dry white wine
½ cup whipping cream

Herb Crust (see recipe opposite)

Butter 4-quart oval baking dish. Place chicken breasts in heavy large pot. Add just enough broth to cover chicken. Bring broth to boil; reduce heat to low. Cover pot and simmer until chicken is just cooked through, skimming surface occasionally, about 20 minutes. Using tongs, transfer chicken to plate and cool.

Add carrots and turnips to broth in pot. Simmer uncovered until just tender, about 10 minutes. Using slotted spoon, transfer vegetables to prepared baking dish. Add turnip greens to broth and cook just until wilted, about 1 minute. Using slotted spoon, transfer greens to colander; drain well. Add to vegetables in dish.

Strain broth; reserve 4 cups. Remove skin and bones from chicken. Cut meat into ¾-inch pieces. Add to vegetables in dish.

Melt butter in same pot over medium heat. Add leeks, shallots and thyme. Sauté until tender, about 8 minutes. Add flour and stir 2 minutes. Stir in 4 cups broth and wine. Increase heat to high and bring to boil, stirring. Add cream and boil until sauce thickens enough to coat spoon, whisking frequently, about 6 minutes. Season with salt and pepper. Pour gravy over mixture in dish. Stir to blend. Cool 45 minutes. *(Can be made 1 day ahead. Cover and chill.)*

Position 1 rack in top third of oven and place baking sheet on bottom rack in oven; preheat to 400°F. Roll out crust dough on parchment paper to 15 x 10½-inch rectangle. Using paper as aid, turn dough over onto filling. Trim overhang; tuck dough edge inside dish. Roll out dough scraps to ¼-inch thickness. Cut out leaf shapes. Brush bottom of cutouts with water; place on crust. Cut slits in crust to allow steam to escape.

Place pot pie on top rack and bake until crust is golden and gravy is bubbling, about 50 minutes. Let stand 10 minutes.

8 SERVINGS

Herb Crust

The best of fall's harvest fills this homestyle pot pie. Make it in a big, colorful casserole that can go straight from the oven to the table.

- 2½ cups all purpose flour
- 2 tablespoons chopped fresh parsley
- 1 tablespoon chopped fresh thyme
- 1 teaspoon salt
- 1 teaspoon sugar
- ½ cup (1 stick) chilled unsalted butter, cut into ½-inch pieces
- ½ cup chilled solid vegetable shortening, cut into ½-inch pieces
- 6½ tablespoons (about) ice water

Blend first 5 ingredients in processor until herbs are very finely chopped. Add butter and shortening. Blend until mixture resembles coarse meal. Transfer mixture to large bowl. Using fork, mix in enough ice water to form moist clumps. Gather dough into ball; flatten into rectangle. Cover and chill 30 minutes. *(Can be made 2 days ahead. Keep chilled. Let soften slightly before rolling out.)*

MAKES 1 CRUST

Chicken, Shrimp and Sausage Paella

spanish paella party for ten

Spanish Olives

Green Salad with Goat Cheese, Artichoke Hearts and Croutons (page 140)

Chicken, Shrimp and Sausage Paella (at right; pictured opposite)

Sangria

Honey Cake from the Bakery

Fresh Fruit

3 tablespoons olive oil
6 fresh Cajun or hot Italian sausages (about 1¾ pounds)
12 chicken thighs with skin and bones (about 4¼ pounds), excess fat trimmed
2 very large onions, chopped (about 5 cups)
10 garlic cloves, chopped, plus 1 garlic clove, minced
12 ounces tomatoes, chopped (about 1½ cups)
2 bay leaves
4 medium zucchini, halved crosswise, then quartered lengthwise (about 1¼ pounds)
3 red bell peppers, cut into 1-inch-wide strips

1½ pounds uncooked large shrimp, peeled, deveined
Generous pinch plus ¼ teaspoon saffron threads

2½ cups arborio rice or medium-grain white rice (about 17½ ounces)
1½ teaspoons salt

5 cups canned low-salt chicken broth
2 teaspoons paprika

Chopped fresh parsley

Heat 1 tablespoon oil in heavy large shallow pot over medium-high heat. Add sausages and sauté until cooked through, turning often, about 10 minutes. Transfer to large bowl. Sprinkle chicken with salt and pepper. Working in batches, add chicken, skin side down, to pot. Cover and cook until brown, about 6 minutes. Turn chicken over, cover and cook until brown and cooked through, about 8 minutes longer. Transfer chicken to bowl with sausages. Add onions and 10 chopped garlic cloves to pot; sauté until tender, about 8 minutes. Add tomatoes and bay leaves; stir 2 minutes. Stir in zucchini and bell peppers. Transfer to another large bowl.

Toss shrimp with remaining 2 tablespoons oil, 1 minced garlic clove and generous pinch of saffron in medium bowl. *(Chicken-sausage mixture, vegetable mixture and shrimp mixture can be prepared 6 hours ahead. Cover separately and refrigerate.)*

Preheat oven to 375°F. Brush one 18 x 12 x 2¼-inch roasting

❖

Do-ahead tips make this rendition of the Spanish classic perfect for entertaining. Traditionally, paella is prepared in a two-handled paella pan on top of the stove, but this recipe conveniently uses a large roasting pan and calls for the dish to be baked.

pan with olive oil. Mix rice and 1½ teaspoons salt into vegetable mixture. Spread rice mixture evenly in prepared pan. Cut sausages diagonally into 1-inch slices. Using wooden spoon, push sausage and chicken pieces into rice mixture; pour any juices from bowl over. Bring broth, paprika and remaining ¼ teaspoon saffron to boil in medium saucepan. Pour evenly over rice mixture. Cover pan tightly with foil. Bake until rice is almost tender, about 40 minutes.

Sprinkle shrimp mixture with salt and pepper. Arrange atop rice mixture. Cover pan with foil; bake until shrimp are opaque in center, rice is tender and most of liquid in pan is absorbed, about 20 minutes longer. Sprinkle with parsley; serve.

10 SERVINGS

Chicken Breasts with Black Bean-Mango Salsa

2 cups ½-inch pieces peeled pitted mangoes
1 15- to 16-ounce can black beans, drained, rinsed
¾ cup fresh white corn kernels
¾ cup finely chopped red onion
½ cup chopped fresh cilantro
3 tablespoons fresh lime juice
1 teaspoon chili oil*
1 teaspoon sugar

⅓ cup yellow cornmeal
1 tablespoon ground coriander
8 5-ounce skinless boneless chicken breasts, excess fat trimmed
Nonstick vegetable oil spray

Place first 8 ingredients in large bowl. Toss to combine. Season salsa with salt and pepper. Cover; let stand 1 hour.

Preheat oven to 250°F. Mix cornmeal and coriander in shallow bowl. Sprinkle chicken with salt and pepper. Generously spray large nonstick skillet with nonstick spray. Place skillet over medium-high heat. Coat 1 side of each chicken breast with cornmeal mixture. Place 4 chicken breasts, cornmeal side down, in skillet; cook until golden on bottom, about 5 minutes. Reduce heat to medium-low. Turn chicken over. Cook chicken until cooked through, about 5 minutes longer. Transfer chicken to baking sheet. Keep warm in oven. Wipe out skillet, then spray with more nonstick spray. Repeat with remaining 4 chicken breasts.

Cut chicken breasts diagonally into ½-inch-thick slices. Transfer to plates. Spoon salsa atop chicken and serve.

**Chili oil is available at Asian markets and in the Asian foods section of some supermarkets.*

8 SERVINGS

south-of-the-border menu for eight

Buttermilk Soup with Cucumber and Crab (page 27)

Chicken Breasts with Black Bean-Mango Salsa (at left; pictured opposite)

Three-Pepper Slaw with Chili Dressing (page 144; pictured opposite)

Corn Bread or Tortillas

Vanilla Ice Cream with Caramel Sauce and Chopped Toasted Almonds

Lemon Butter Cookies (page 197)

Sage-roasted Turkey with Caramelized Onions and Sage Gravy

The gravy for this succulent roasted turkey features sweet caramelized onions along with fresh sage and a pinch of nutmeg. Garnish the bird with sage sprigs, kumquats and cranberries, if you like.

1½ pounds onions, sliced
3 tablespoons vegetable oil

1 14- to 15-pound turkey, neck and giblets reserved and cut into 1-inch pieces
2 tablespoons (¼ stick) butter, room temperature
8 large whole fresh sage leaves plus 1½ teaspoons chopped

1 cup (or more) canned low-salt chicken broth

6 tablespoons all purpose flour
¾ cup dry white wine
Pinch of ground nutmeg

Position rack in bottom third of oven and preheat to 425°F. Toss onions and 2 tablespoons oil in large roasting pan. Roast until onions are golden brown, stirring every 15 minutes, about 1 hour.

Meanwhile, rinse turkey inside and out; pat dry. Slide hand under skin of turkey breast to loosen skin. Spread butter under skin over breast meat. Arrange 4 sage leaves under skin on each side of breast. Tuck wing tips under turkey; tie legs together loosely to hold shape. Rub turkey all over with remaining 1 tablespoon oil; sprinkle turkey with salt and pepper.

Place turkey atop onions in pan. Add neck and giblet pieces to pan. Roast turkey 30 minutes. Pour 1 cup broth into pan. Tent turkey loosely with foil. Reduce oven temperature to 325°F. Roast turkey 2 hours. Uncover; continue to roast until turkey is golden brown and thermometer inserted into thickest part of thigh registers 180°F, basting occasionally with pan juices, about 1 hour longer. Transfer turkey to platter. Tent loosely with foil; let stand 30 minutes.

Remove giblet pieces from roasting pan. Pour onion mixture into large glass measuring cup; spoon off fat, reserving 2 tablespoons. Add more broth to onion mixture, if necessary, to measure 5 cups.

Heat reserved 2 tablespoons turkey fat in heavy large saucepan over medium-high heat. Add chopped sage and stir until fragrant, about 30 seconds. Add flour; whisk until beginning to color, about 3 minutes (mixture will be dry and crumbly). Gradually whisk in onion mixture, wine and nutmeg. Simmer until gravy thickens, whisking frequently, about 5 minutes; season with salt and pepper.

Carve turkey and serve with gravy.

10 TO 12 SERVINGS

Lemon-Sage Cornish Game Hens with Tomato-Porcini Sauce

italian-style dinner for four

Antipasto Platter

Lemon-Sage Cornish Game Hens with Tomato-Porcini Sauce (at right; pictured opposite)

Soft Polenta with Leeks (opposite; pictured opposite)

Chianti

Poached Pears

Chocolate-dipped Biscotti

Espresso

- ¾ cup hot water
- ¾ ounce dried porcini mushrooms*

- 4 tablespoons olive oil
- 1 tablespoon plus 4 teaspoons chopped fresh sage
- 2 garlic cloves, minced
- 1 14½-ounce can whole peeled tomatoes in juice, pureed in blender with juices
- ½ cup canned low-salt chicken broth

- 4 1¼- to 1½-pound Cornish game hens, giblets removed
- 4 large fresh sage sprigs
- 1 lemon, cut into 4 wedges
- Soft Polenta with Leeks (see recipe opposite)

Combine ¾ cup hot water and porcini mushrooms in small bowl. Let stand until mushrooms soften, about 30 minutes. Using slotted spoon, transfer mushrooms to work surface. Coarsely chop mushrooms. Set mushrooms and soaking liquid aside.

Heat 2 tablespoons oil in heavy medium skillet over medium heat. Add 1 tablespoon chopped sage and garlic. Sauté until fragrant, about 1 minute. Add pureed tomatoes, broth, chopped mushrooms and soaking liquid, leaving any sediment from liquid behind. Simmer over medium-low heat until thickened to sauce consistency, about 25 minutes. *(Sauce can be made 1 day ahead. Cover; chill.)*

Preheat oven to 450°F. Pat hens dry with paper towels. Sprinkle cavities with salt and pepper. Place 1 sage sprig and 1 lemon wedge in cavity of each hen. Tie legs together. Tuck wing tips under hen. Place hens on rack in large roasting pan. Rub remaining 2 tablespoons oil over hens. Sprinkle with salt and pepper. Sprinkle 1 teaspoon chopped sage over breast of each hen. Roast until hens are cooked through and juices run clear when thickest part of thigh is pierced, about 50 minutes. Transfer hens to platter. Tent with foil.

Pour pan juices from roasting pan into 1-cup glass measuring cup, scraping up any browned bits from bottom of pan. Spoon fat off top of juices. Add pan juices to tomato sauce. Simmer 2 minutes to blend flavors. Season sauce to taste with salt and pepper.

Spoon polenta onto plates. Spoon sauce over. Place hens atop.

**Dried porcini mushrooms are available at Italian markets, specialty foods stores and many supermarkets.*

4 SERVINGS

If you can find it, use stone-ground coarse cornmeal for the polenta; it's grainier than regular cornmeal and gives the dish an appealing, slightly crackly texture.

Soft Polenta with Leeks

- 3 tablespoons butter
- 3 large leeks (white and pale green parts only), thinly sliced
- 2¼ cups (or more) water
- 2 cups canned chicken broth
- 1 bay leaf
- 1 cup polenta (coarse cornmeal)*
- ⅓ cup freshly grated Parmesan cheese

Melt 2 tablespoons butter in heavy large saucepan over medium heat. Add leeks; stir to coat. Cover and cook until leeks soften, stirring occasionally, about 10 minutes. Add 2¼ cups water, broth and bay leaf. Bring to boil. Gradually whisk in polenta. Reduce heat to medium-low and cook until mixture is thick and creamy, stirring often and thinning with more water if necessary, about 35 minutes.

Remove pan from heat. Discard bay leaf. Stir in remaining 1 tablespoon butter and Parmesan cheese. Season polenta to taste with salt and pepper. Divide polenta among plates.

**Sold at Italian markets, natural foods stores and some supermarkets. If unavailable, substitute 1 cup regular yellow cornmeal, and cook leek-cornmeal mixture only about 15 minutes.*

4 SERVINGS

Red Snapper with Potatoes, Tomatoes and Red Wine

greek menu
for six

Ouzo

Marinated Olives and Feta Cheese
(page 18)

Herbed Eggplant Spread
(page 19)

Red Snapper with
Potatoes, Tomatoes and Red Wine
(at right; pictured opposite)

Pinot Noir

Fresh Fruit with Rose Water Syrup
(page 162)

- 4 large Yukon Gold potatoes, peeled, cut into ¼-inch-thick slices

- 1 tablespoon butter
- 9 tablespoons extra-virgin olive oil
- 3 small onions, sliced
- 8 garlic cloves, thinly sliced
- 1 cup dry red wine
- 2 cups chicken stock or canned low-salt chicken broth
- 1 14½-ounce can diced tomatoes in juice
- 1 teaspoon dried oregano
- ⅓ cup Kalamata olives or other brine-cured black olives
- 4 tablespoons chopped fresh parsley

- 6 7-ounce red snapper or blackfish fillets

Steam potatoes until almost tender, about 8 minutes. Cool.

Melt butter with 2 tablespoons oil in heavy large pot over medium-high heat. Add onions; sauté until golden brown, about 8 minutes. Mix in 3 tablespoons oil and sliced garlic. Add potatoes; cook 2 minutes. Mix in red wine. Boil until almost no liquid remains, about 4 minutes. Add stock, tomatoes with juices and oregano and bring to boil. Add olives; boil until liquid thickens slightly and potatoes are very tender, about 12 minutes. Mix in 3 tablespoons parsley. Season with salt and pepper.

Meanwhile, sprinkle fish with salt and pepper. Heat 1½ tablespoons oil in each of 2 heavy large nonstick skillets over medium-high heat. Add fish; sauté until opaque in center, 3 minutes per side.

Arrange potatoes in center of each of 6 plates. Spoon some sauce over. Top with fish. Spoon remaining sauce over fish. Sprinkle with 1 tablespoon parsley. Drizzle with 1 tablespoon olive oil and serve.

6 SERVINGS

friday night
dinner for two

Dilled Cucumber Salad

Seared Salmon on Baby Spinach
(at right; pictured at right)

Steamed Squash

French Bread

Sauvignon Blanc

Chocolate Mousse

Seared Salmon on Baby Spinach

- 2 7-ounce skinless salmon fillets
- 2 tablespoons (¼ stick) butter
- 3 large shallots, sliced
- 1½ tablespoons chopped fresh tarragon
- 3 ounces baby spinach leaves
- ⅓ cup dry white wine
- ¼ cup whipping cream

Sprinkle salmon with salt and pepper. Melt 1 tablespoon butter in medium skillet over medium-high heat. Add salmon; sauté until just opaque in center, about 4 minutes per side. Transfer to plate.

Melt ½ tablespoon butter in same skillet. Add half of shallots and half of tarragon; sauté 30 seconds. Increase heat to high; add half of spinach and toss 30 seconds. Add remaining spinach; toss until wilted. Divide between plates.

Melt remaining ½ tablespoon butter in same skillet over medium-high heat. Add remaining shallots and tarragon; sauté 30 seconds. Add wine and cream and boil until sauce is thick enough to coat spoon, about 3 minutes. Season with salt and pepper. Return salmon to skillet; simmer 1 minute. Arrange salmon atop spinach. Spoon shallot-wine sauce over salmon and serve.

2 SERVINGS

Tuna, Tomato, Olive and Artichoke Sandwiches

- 3 4-inch-wide 24-inch-long French-bread bâtards
- 5 medium tomatoes, quartered
- ¼ cup plus 6 tablespoons olive oil
- 2 tablespoons red wine vinegar
- 3 garlic cloves
- 6 large tomatoes, sliced
- 3 6- to 6½-ounce jars marinated artichoke hearts, drained, sliced
- 1 cup Kalamata olives, pitted, halved
- 2 2-ounce cans anchovies, drained
- ½ bunch celery, sliced
- 1 bunch radishes, sliced
- 1 bunch green onions, chopped
- 4 6-ounce cans solid white tuna packed in oil, drained, flaked
- 6 bunches arugula

Cut breads lengthwise in half. Scoop out insides, leaving ½-inch-thick shell. Puree quartered tomatoes, ¼ cup oil, vinegar and garlic in processor. Brush ⅓ cup dressing over each bread half. Arrange sliced tomatoes, artichokes, olives and anchovies over bottom halves. Top with celery, radishes and onions, then tuna and arugula. Drizzle each sandwich with 2 tablespoons oil. Sprinkle with salt and pepper. Press top halves over. Press firmly. Wrap in foil; chill 1 to 3 hours. Cut each sandwich into 4 sections.

12 SERVINGS

This tuna sandwich has the basic components of a *salade niçoise.* In France, the sandwich is referred to as *pan bagnat,* which translates to "wet bread." In other words, provide extra napkins if you plan to pack this along on a picnic lunch.

Cod with Miso Glaze and Wasabi Mashed Potatoes

- ½ cup light yellow miso (fermented soybean paste)
- 5 tablespoons rice vinegar
- ¼ cup sugar
- 2 tablespoons soy sauce
- ¼ teaspoon cayenne pepper
- ¼ cup vegetable oil
- 6 6-ounce cod fillets, each cut into 2 pieces

Wasabi Mashed Potatoes (see recipe below)

The fermented soybean paste called miso and wasabi powder, also known as horseradish powder, are available at Japanese markets, specialty foods stores and in the Asian foods section of some supermarkets.

Preheat broiler. Blend miso, vinegar, sugar, soy and cayenne in processor. With machine running, gradually pour in oil; blend until mixture is smooth. Place cod in large bowl. Pour half of miso mixture over fish; toss to coat. Transfer to rimmed baking sheet.

Broil cod 8 inches from heat until beginning to brown, about 3 minutes. Set oven at 450°F; bake cod until opaque in center, about 5 minutes. Divide cod among 6 plates. Spoon mashed potatoes alongside. Drizzle remaining miso mixture over cod and potatoes.

6 SERVINGS

Wasabi Mashed Potatoes

- 3 pounds russet potatoes, peeled, cut into 2-inch pieces
- ¾ cup whole milk
- 1 tablespoon wasabi powder (horseradish powder)
- ¼ cup (½ stick) butter

Place potatoes in large pot of cold salted water. Boil until tender, about 20 minutes. Drain. Return to pot; mash.

Combine ¾ cup milk and 1 tablespoon wasabi powder in small bowl. Stir to dissolve powder. Add milk mixture and butter to potatoes. Using electric mixer, beat until fluffy and smooth. Season with salt and pepper. *(Can be prepared 2 hours ahead. Cover; keep at room temperature. Rewarm over low heat, stirring.)*

6 SERVINGS

Grilled Trout with Lemon-Sage Butter

¾ cup (1½ sticks) butter
2½ tablespoons grated lemon peel
1½ tablespoons chopped fresh sage

12 trout fillets, butterflied
Fresh lemon wedges

Melt butter in heavy small saucepan over medium-low heat. Remove from heat. Add lemon peel and chopped fresh sage. Season to taste with salt and pepper.

Prepare barbecue (medium-high heat). Brush flesh and skin sides of fish with butter mixture. Sprinkle with salt and pepper. Close fish; secure with toothpicks. Grill until just opaque in center, about 4 minutes per side. Remove toothpicks. Serve, passing lemon wedges.

12 SERVINGS

dinner on the patio for twelve

Asparagus and Sugar Snap Peas with Honey-Mustard Dip (page 23)

Grilled Trout with Lemon-Sage Butter (at left; pictured at left)

Red Potato Salad with Onions and Olives (page 144; pictured at left)

Green Bean and Shiitake Mushroom Salad (page 145; pictured at left)

Country Bread

Chardonnay

Apricot-Almond Tarts (page 159)

Grilled Salmon with Tomato, Cucumber and Caper Salsa

- ⅓ cup fresh lemon juice
- ⅓ cup extra-virgin olive oil
- ⅓ cup chopped shallots
- 1 tablespoon grated lemon peel
- 1¾ teaspoons ground cumin

- 1 medium English hothouse cucumber, unpeeled, diced
- 1 12-ounce basket small cherry tomatoes, each quartered
- 1 large yellow bell pepper, diced
- ¼ cup drained capers
- 2 tablespoons chopped fresh cilantro

Nonstick vegetable oil spray
- 1 2½- to 2¾-pound salmon fillet with skin (1 whole side)

Whisk lemon juice, olive oil, shallots, peel and cumin in small bowl. Season marinade with salt and pepper.

Combine ½ cup marinade, cucumber and next 4 ingredients in medium bowl; season salsa to taste with salt and pepper. Let stand 30 minutes; toss occasionally.

Spray barbecue rack with nonstick spray and prepare barbecue (medium-high heat). Place salmon, skin side down, in large glass baking dish. Top with remaining marinade. Let stand 10 minutes. Sprinkle with salt and pepper.

TO GRILL SALMON USING FISH BASKET: Spray basket with nonstick spray. Place salmon in fish basket, folding tail under if fish is too long. Place basket on barbecue and grill salmon, skin side up, 5 minutes. Turn basket over; grill salmon until just opaque in center, about 5 minutes longer. Turn salmon out onto platter.

TO GRILL SALMON WITHOUT USING A BASKET: Spray rimless baking sheet with nonstick spray. Place salmon, skin side up, on sheet. Spray skin with nonstick spray. Slide salmon, skin side up, onto barbecue. Grill 5 minutes. Stand blade of large spatula at 1 long side of salmon to hold in place. From opposite side, slide rimless baking sheet completely under salmon. Hold salmon with spatula; turn sheet and salmon over, releasing salmon, skin side down, onto barbecue. Grill salmon until just opaque in center, about 5 minutes longer. Slide baking sheet under salmon; transfer fish to platter. Serve with salsa.

8 SERVINGS

To turn salmon without using a basket: Stand the blade of a large metal spatula along one side of the salmon to keep it from moving around. From the opposite side, slide a rimless baking sheet under the salmon, and lift the fish off the barbecue.

Using the spatula to hold the salmon in place on the baking sheet, gently flip the fish, skin side down, onto the barbecue.

Fish Soup with Tomatoes and Red Pepper-Garlic Sauce

Tomatoes are a key ingredient in this delicately flavored fish soup. The Provençal spread *rouille,* a pungent garlic and bell pepper condiment named for its burnished red color, adds interest.

❖

SOUP

- 2 tablespoons extra-virgin olive oil
- 1 medium onion, finely chopped
- 1 fennel bulb, coarsely chopped
- 8 cups fish stock or bottled clam juice
- 1 cup chopped fresh Italian parsley
- 2 3-inch-long strips orange peel
- 3 pounds ripe tomatoes, peeled, coarsely chopped
- 1 pound medium-size red-skinned potatoes, peeled, cut into ¼-inch-thick rounds
- 1 large red-skinned potato, quartered
- 1 large pinch of saffron threads

ROUILLE

- 1 red bell pepper

- 6 tablespoons extra-virgin olive oil
- 3 garlic cloves

- 1 French-bread baguette, cut into ¼-inch-thick rounds

- 2½ pounds lingcod fillets or red snapper fillets, cut into 1½-inch pieces

FOR SOUP: Heat oil in large pot over medium heat. Add onion and fennel. Sauté until onion is translucent, 8 minutes. Add stock, parsley and peel. Bring to boil. Reduce heat; cover and simmer until fennel is tender, about 5 minutes. Add tomatoes, sliced potatoes, quartered potato and saffron. Cover partially; simmer until potatoes are tender, about 12 minutes. Remove from heat.

Remove quartered potato from soup. Cool slightly. Peel potato; discard skin. Transfer to processor.

FOR ROUILLE: Char bell pepper over gas flame or in broiler until blackened on all sides. Enclose pepper in paper bag 10 minutes to steam. Peel and seed pepper. Cool.

Transfer bell pepper to processor with potato. Add 2 tablespoons oil and garlic. Process until smooth. With machine running, gradually blend in 4 tablespoons oil. Season with salt.

Preheat broiler. Arrange bread rounds on baking sheet. Broil until crisp, about 2 minutes. *(Can be made 1 day ahead. Cover soup and rouille separately; chill. Cool toasts, then store airtight at room temperature. Bring soup to simmer before continuing.)*

Add fish to soup. Simmer until fish is just opaque in center, 5 minutes. Spoon rouille onto 12 to 16 toasts. Ladle soup into bowls. Top each with 2 toasts. Pass remaining toasts and rouille.

6 TO 8 SERVINGS

Chili-seasoned Fish Sticks

Nonstick vegetable oil spray
6 tablespoons all purpose flour
3 tablespoons yellow cornmeal
1¾ teaspoons chili powder
⅓ cup mayonnaise
2 tablespoons fresh lemon juice
12 ounces firm white fish fillets (such as orange roughy or halibut), cut crosswise into ¾-inch-wide strips

Position rack in top third of oven and preheat to 500°F. Spray small baking sheet with nonstick vegetable oil spray. Whisk all purpose flour, yellow cornmeal and chili powder in shallow dish to blend. Stir mayonnaise and fresh lemon juice in another shallow dish to blend. Sprinkle fish fillets on all sides with salt and pepper. Dip fish fillets into mayonnaise mixture, then into flour mixture to coat completely. Arrange fish on prepared sheet. Bake until coating is crisp and golden and fish is cooked through, about 10 minutes.

2 SERVINGS

There's no need to buy ordinary frozen fish sticks at the market when you can make this version, updated with a spicy hint of chili powder, in under 30 minutes.

Seafood and Turkey-Sausage Gumbo

mardi gras menu for four

Oysters on the Half Shell with Hot Sauce

Seafood and Turkey-Sausage Gumbo (at right; pictured above)

Spicy Rice and Kale (page 131; pictured above)

Beer

Pecan Pie from the Bakery

- ¼ cup all purpose flour

- 1 tablespoon vegetable oil
- 1 cup chopped onion
- 1 cup chopped green bell pepper
- 3 garlic cloves, chopped
- 1 teaspoon dried thyme
- 1 bay leaf
- 3 low-fat Italian turkey sausages (about 10 ounces), casings removed
- 1 28-ounce can diced tomatoes in juice
- 1 cup canned low-salt chicken broth or vegetable broth
- 2 teaspoons Creole or Cajun seasoning

- 8 uncooked large shrimp, peeled, deveined
- 2 6-ounce catfish fillets, each cut into 4 pieces

Sprinkle flour over bottom of heavy large pot. Stir flour constantly over medium-low heat until flour turns golden brown (do not allow to burn), about 15 minutes. Pour browned flour into bowl.

Heat oil in same pot over medium heat. Add onion and bell pepper and sauté until tender, about 7 minutes. Add garlic, thyme and bay leaf; stir 1 minute. Add sausages and sauté until brown, breaking up with back of spoon, about 5 minutes. Stir in browned flour, tomatoes with juices, then chicken broth and Creole seasoning. Bring to boil. Reduce heat, cover pot and simmer gumbo 20 minutes to blend flavors, stirring frequently.

Add shrimp and catfish to pot and simmer just until seafood is opaque in center, about 5 minutes. Discard bay leaf. Season to taste with salt and pepper and then serve.

4 SERVINGS

Asian-Style Crab and Shrimp Cakes

¼ cup mayonnaise
2 tablespoons chopped fresh cilantro
1 tablespoon chopped peeled fresh ginger
2 teaspoons bottled Thai fish sauce (nam pla) or soy sauce
6 ounces canned crabmeat, drained, picked over, patted dry
3 ounces bay shrimp, chopped
1½ cups fresh breadcrumbs made from crustless French bread

1½ tablespoons peanut oil

Blend first 4 ingredients in medium bowl. Mix in crabmeat, shrimp and ½ cup breadcrumbs. Season with pepper. Place remaining 1 cup breadcrumbs on plate. Drop ¼ of crab mixture into breadcrumbs; turn to coat. Shape into 2½-inch-diameter cake. Repeat coating and shaping with remaining crab mixture and crumbs, forming total of 4 cakes.

Heat oil in heavy medium skillet over medium heat. Add cakes and sauté until crisp, about 5 minutes per side.

2 SERVINGS

Open-face Lobster Salad Sandwiches

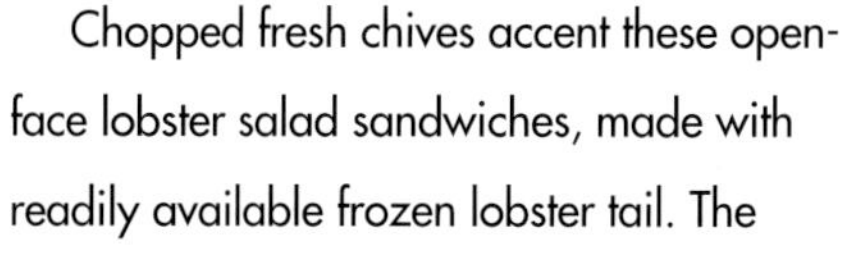
Chopped fresh chives accent these open-face lobster salad sandwiches, made with readily available frozen lobster tail. The recipe doubles—or triples—easily.

¼ cup mayonnaise
¼ cup finely chopped celery
1 teaspoon fresh lemon juice
½ teaspoon grated lemon peel
3 tablespoons chopped fresh chives
1 11- to 12-ounce frozen lobster tail, thawed

4 slices egg bread, toasted

Combine first 4 ingredients and 2 tablespoons chives in medium bowl. Cook lobster in medium pot of boiling salted water until just opaque in center, about 8 minutes. Drain; cool. Remove lobster meat from shell. Dice lobster; fold into mayonnaise mixture. Season to taste with salt and pepper.

Spoon lobster salad atop bread slices. Sprinkle with remaining 1 tablespoon chives and serve.

2 SERVINGS

Steamed Mussels with Pernod, Celery Root and Saffron Aioli

seafood supper for six

Brine-cured Black Olives

Arugula, Fennel and Orange Salad (page 141)

Steamed Mussels with Pernod, Celery Root and Saffron Aioli (at right; pictured opposite)

Crusty Bread

Sauvignon Blanc

Tropical Fruit Compote with Mango Sorbet (page 165; pictured opposite)

AIOLI

1 tablespoon hot water
Pinch of saffron threads, crumbled
⅔ cup low-fat mayonnaise
2 garlic cloves, minced

MUSSELS

2 tablespoons olive oil
1 large celery root, peeled, finely chopped (about 2½ cups)
1 large leek (white and pale green parts only), thinly sliced
2 carrots, peeled, finely chopped
2 celery stalks, finely chopped
6 tablespoons finely chopped fresh parsley
4 garlic cloves, minced
4½ pounds mussels, scrubbed, debearded
1½ cups dry white wine
⅓ cup Pernod or other anise-flavored liqueur

FOR AIOLI: Combine 1 tablespoon hot water and saffron in medium bowl. Let stand 5 minutes. Whisk in mayonnaise and garlic. Season with salt. *(Can be made 1 day ahead. Cover; chill.)*

FOR MUSSELS: Heat 2 tablespoons olive oil in heavy large pot over medium heat. Add celery root, leek, carrots, chopped celery and 4 tablespoons parsley. Stir to coat. Cover pot and cook until vegetables are tender, stirring occasionally, about 15 minutes. Add garlic and sauté 1 minute. Add mussels, wine and Pernod. Increase heat to high. Cover and cook until mussels open, stirring occasionally, about 6 minutes (discard any mussels that do not open). Remove from heat. Season cooking liquid to taste with salt and pepper.

Whisk ½ cup cooking liquid into aioli to make thin sauce. Ladle mussels and remaining cooking liquid into 6 bowls. Drizzle each serving with some aioli. Sprinkle with remaining 2 tablespoons parsley. Serve mussels, passing remaining aioli separately.

6 SERVINGS

Orange and Roasted Garlic Shrimp Skewers

low-fat dinner for six

Orange and Roasted Garlic Shrimp Skewers (at right; pictured at right)

Risotto-Style Barley with Spring Greens (page 130; pictured at right)

Pinot Grigio

Poached Pears with Sweet Wine and Fruit Confetti (page 167)

- 20 large garlic cloves, unpeeled
- ¼ cup dry white wine

- 2 cups orange juice
- 60 medium uncooked shrimp (about 1¾ pounds), peeled, deveined, shells reserved

- 12 6-inch-long wooden skewers, soaked in water, drained
- ¾ cup chopped fresh Italian parsley

Nonstick vegetable oil spray

Preheat oven to 325°F. Place garlic and wine in center of foil sheet. Sprinkle with salt and pepper. Enclose with foil; crimp edges to seal. Bake until garlic is very tender, about 50 minutes. Squeeze garlic between fingers to release cloves. Transfer garlic cloves and any remaining cooking liquid to blender.

Meanwhile, combine orange juice and reserved shrimp shells in heavy medium saucepan. Boil until liquid is reduced to ¾ cup, about 10 minutes. Strain liquid into blender with garlic; discard shrimp shells. Puree until mixture is smooth. Cool marinade.

Mix shrimp and marinade in large bowl. Cover and refrigerate for 1½ hours. Drain marinade.

Thread 5 shrimp onto each skewer. Place parsley in shallow dish. Coat 1 side of each shrimp skewer with parsley.

Spray large nonstick skillet with nonstick spray. Place skillet over medium-high heat. Add 6 shrimp skewers to skillet, parsley side down; cook until shrimp are pink and just cooked through, about 1½ minutes per side. Wipe out skillet, then spray with more nonstick spray. Repeat with remaining 6 shrimp skewers. Serve.

6 SERVINGS

Baked Scallops with Herbed Breadcrumb Topping

Tender and sweet bay scallops star in this surprisingly sophisticated entrée for two, which can be prepared in under 30 minutes. Pass lemon wedges alongside.

- 2 tablespoons (¼ stick) butter
- 12 ounces bay scallops
- 1 cup fresh breadcrumbs made from crustless French bread
- 1 large garlic clove, minced
- 2 tablespoons chopped fresh parsley
- 1 tablespoon chopped fresh tarragon

Lemon wedges

Preheat oven to 450°F. Melt butter in heavy medium skillet. Brush 10-inch-diameter glass pie dish with some of butter. Place scallops in single layer in prepared dish. Sprinkle with salt and pepper. Add breadcrumbs and garlic to remaining butter in skillet. Stir over medium heat until crumbs are crisp, about 5 minutes. Mix in parsley and tarragon. Top scallops with crumb mixture.

Bake scallops until topping is golden and scallops are opaque in center, about 10 minutes. Serve with lemon wedges.

2 SERVINGS

Meatless Tamale Pie

1 pound poblano chilies*

2 tablespoons olive oil
4½ cups frozen corn kernels
1 to 2 jalapeño chilies, seeded, finely chopped
2 garlic cloves, chopped
1½ teaspoons ground cumin
1½ teaspoons dried oregano
1 14½-ounce can diced tomatoes in juice, drained, ¾ cup juice reserved
¾ cup thinly sliced green onions
½ cup chopped fresh cilantro

1 2-pound butternut squash, peeled, halved lengthwise, seeded, cut crosswise into ½-inch-thick slices
1½ cups shredded sharp cheddar cheese
1½ cups shredded Monterey Jack cheese

7 cups water
1½ teaspoons salt
2 cups yellow cornmeal
1 cup plain yogurt

2 tomatoes, sliced

Fresh cilantro sprigs

❖

No one will miss the meat in this vegetarian tamale pie with corn, tomatoes, butternut squash and plenty of cheese. Look for dark green *poblano* chilies for this recipe—they lend the richest flavor.

❖

Roast poblano chilies over gas flame or in broiler until blackened on all sides. Enclose chilies in paper bag. Let stand 10 minutes. Peel, seed and coarsely chop chilies.

Heat 2 tablespoons olive oil in heavy large skillet over medium-high heat. Add corn kernels and cook until beginning to brown, stirring occasionally, about 5 minutes. Add jalapeño chilies, garlic, cumin and oregano; sauté 2 minutes. Remove from heat. Mix in roasted poblano chilies, canned tomatoes, ½ cup reserved juice from canned tomatoes, green onions and cilantro. Season with salt and pepper.

Cook squash in large pot of boiling salted water until crisp-tender, about 4 minutes. Drain. Mix cheeses in medium bowl.

Preheat oven to 350°F. Lightly oil 15 x 10 x 2-inch glass baking dish. Combine 5 cups water and 1½ teaspoons salt in heavy large saucepan. Bring to boil. Combine cornmeal and remaining 2 cups water in another medium bowl. Gradually whisk cornmeal mixture into boiling salted water. Reduce heat to medium-low. Cook until cornmeal is very tender and mixture is thick, stirring often, about 14 minutes. Remove from heat and mix in yogurt.

Spread ⅔ of cornmeal over bottom of prepared dish (cover remaining cornmeal to keep warm). Arrange squash over cornmeal in dish. Sprinkle squash with salt and pepper. Sprinkle 2 cups cheese over squash. Spoon corn kernel mixture evenly over cheese, spreading with spatula. Spread remaining cornmeal evenly over corn kernel mixture. Arrange tomato slices atop cornmeal, pressing gently. Sprinkle with salt and pepper. Drizzle remaining ¼ cup juice from canned tomatoes over. Sprinkle remaining cheese over casserole.

Bake casserole uncovered until heated through and top is golden, about 1 hour. *(Can be made 1 day ahead. Cool slightly. Cover and refrigerate. Rewarm, covered with foil, in 350°F oven until heated through, about 30 minutes.)*

Let casserole stand 15 minutes. Garnish with cilantro sprigs.

**Fresh green chilies, often called* pasillas; *available at Latin American markets and some supermarkets.*

8 SERVINGS

vegetarian supper for eight

Guacamole with Tortilla Chips

Meatless Tamale Pie (opposite; pictured at left)

Romaine Salad with Red Wine Vinaigrette

Purchased Coffee Ice Cream with Fudge Sauce

vitamins: an a-to-k guide

Doctors agree: A varied diet with generous amounts of grains, fruits and vegetables and moderate amounts of meat and dairy products can more than adequately deliver the doses we need of the vitamins that have been found to defend against heart disease, cancer and more. Here's what you need to eat:

- A (retinol or beta-carotene): Essential for growth, healthy skin, good vision, strong immune system. Sources: liver; eggs; margarine; whole and fortified low-fat milk; orange, yellow and red fruits and vegetables.
- B_1 (thiamine): Helps convert carbohydrates to energy. Sources: unrefined cereal, grains, pork, liver, beans, nuts.
- B_2 (riboflavin): See B_1; also helps form red blood cells and keep skin and eyes healthy. Sources: meat, poultry, eggs, dairy products, dark green vegetables such as spinach and broccoli.
- B_3 (niacin): Converts fats and proteins into energy; helps keep skin, digestion and nerves healthy; lowers high blood-cholesterol levels. Sources: fortified cereal and flour, legumes, meat, peanut butter.
- B_6 (pyridoxine): Removes heart-disease-causing homocysteine from blood; metabolizes protein; helps form red blood cells. Sources: fish, meat, poultry,

Mediterranean Salad

2 cups ½-inch pieces peeled white potatoes (about 1 pound)
1 cup ½-inch pieces peeled carrots
1 cup ½-inch pieces fennel bulb (about 1 medium), fronds reserved
1 15- to 16-ounce can garbanzo beans (chickpeas), rinsed, drained
½ cup ½-inch pieces red onion
1 7-ounce jar roasted red peppers, drained, chopped
½ cup chopped fresh parsley

4 tablespoons red wine vinegar
3 tablespoons olive oil
1 garlic clove, minced

4 hard-boiled eggs, peeled

Cook potatoes in medium pot of boiling salted water 4 minutes. Add carrots and cook until all vegetables are crisp-tender, about 4 minutes longer. Drain. Rinse vegetables under cold water. Drain well. Combine potatoes, carrots, fennel bulb, garbanzo beans, red onion, roasted peppers and parsley in large bowl.

Whisk red wine vinegar, olive oil and minced garlic in small bowl. Add to salad; toss to coat.

Cut eggs in half lengthwise. Separate yolks from whites (reserve 2 yolks for another use). Chop egg whites; mix into salad. Season with salt and pepper. Mound salad in serving bowl. Crumble remaining 2 yolks over salad. Garnish with fennel fronds. Serve at room temperature or cover and chill up to 4 hours.

4 SERVINGS

Toasted Almond Tofu Burgers

1 12-ounce package firm tofu, drained, patted dry, cut into 1-inch-thick slices

Nonstick vegetable oil spray
½ cup grated carrot
½ cup thinly sliced green onions
2 teaspoons minced peeled fresh ginger
1 garlic clove, minced
½ cup almonds, toasted, finely chopped
1 large egg white, beaten to blend
4 teaspoons soy sauce

1 teaspoon oriental sesame oil
1 teaspoon sesame seeds, toasted

4 sesame seed buns, toasted
4 tomato slices
1 cup alfalfa sprouts

Wrap tofu in doubled dish towel. Place on work surface. Weigh down with a board topped with food cans for about 1 hour. Squeeze towel-wrapped tofu to extract as much liquid as possible. Transfer tofu to bowl. Using fork, mash into small pieces.

Spray medium nonstick skillet with nonstick spray; place over medium heat. Add carrot, green onions, ginger and garlic; sauté until slightly softened, about 3 minutes. Cool. Mix carrot mixture, almonds, egg white, soy sauce, sesame oil and sesame seeds into tofu. Season with salt and pepper. Shape into four ½-inch-thick patties.

If grilling, spray grill rack with nonstick spray, then prepare barbecue (medium heat). If sautéing, spray large nonstick skillet with nonstick spray and heat over medium heat. Lightly spray patties on both sides with nonstick spray. Place patties on grill or in skillet and cook until golden brown and heated through, about 3 minutes per side.

Place 1 burger on each bun bottom. Top each with 1 tomato slice, some sprouts and bun top and serve.

4 SERVINGS

vitamins: an a-to-k guide

legumes, unprocessed whole grains, potatoes, nuts, avocados, bananas.

- B_{12} (cobalamin): Helps form red blood cells. Sources: meat, fish, poultry, eggs, milk, fortified soy milk.
- C (ascorbic acid): Maintains healthy tissues and bones; assists in healing; destroys free radicals; and protects immune system. Sources: fruits (especially citrus, strawberries and fresh currants), broccoli and tomatoes.
- D: Works along with calcium to keep bones and teeth healthy. Sources: fortified dairy products and oily fish, such as salmon and tuna.
- E: Essential for healthy function of nervous, muscular, reproductive and immune systems. May help prevent prostate cancer and heart disease. Sources: vegetable oil, peanut butter, liver, whole grains, nuts, leafy greens.
- Folic Acid (folate): This B vitamin plays a crucial role in preventing birth defects; breaks down amino acids to build red blood cells; may give protection from some forms of cancer and heart disease. Sources: dried beans, lentils, liver, nuts, whole grains, dark leafy greens, some fortified breads and breakfast cereals.
- K: Helps blood to clot; also useful in making bone and kidney tissues. Sources: cheese, liver, milk, eggs, greens.

Vegetable Ragout with Parmesan and Balsamic Vinegar

A splash of balsamic vinegar flavors a delicious "stew" of artichokes, carrots, cherry tomatoes, mushrooms, peas and baby lima beans. Shavings of Parmesan top it off.

- 2 lemons, halved
- 8 artichokes (about 9 to 12 ounces each)

- 28 baby carrots, greens trimmed (about 4 bunches)

- ¼ cup olive oil
- 24 cherry tomatoes (about 1 pound), halved
- 12 ounces button mushrooms, halved
- 1 10-ounce package frozen baby peas, thawed
- 1 10-ounce package frozen baby lima beans, thawed
- ¼ cup (½ stick) unsalted butter

- 2 tablespoons balsamic vinegar
- 3 ounces Parmesan cheese, cut into thin shavings

Squeeze juice from lemons into large pot; add lemons. Fill pot with water. Cut stem and top ⅓ from 1 artichoke. Starting at base, bend leaves back and snap off where they break naturally; continue until all tough outer leaves have been removed. Using small knife, trim outside of base until smooth and no dark green areas remain. Cut artichoke lengthwise into quarters. Cut out choke from quarters. Cut each quarter in half, making ½-inch wedges. Place artichoke pieces in lemon water. Repeat with remaining artichokes. Cover pot and bring to boil. Boil artichokes until tender, about 10 minutes. Drain; set aside. *(Can be made 1 day ahead. Cover; chill.)*

Cook carrots in large pot of boiling water 5 minutes. Drain well. *(Carrots can be made 1 day ahead. Cover; chill.)*

Heat ¼ cup olive oil in heavy large pot over medium-high heat. Add tomatoes and mushrooms. Sauté until tomatoes and mushrooms release juices, about 8 minutes. Add artichokes, carrots, baby peas and lima beans. Cook until lima beans and peas are tender and juices thicken slightly, stirring often, about 10 minutes. Add ¼ cup butter and stir until melted. Season vegetables with salt and pepper.

Transfer ragout to large bowl. Toss with balsamic vinegar and sprinkle with Parmesan shavings.

4 SERVINGS

Brie and Mushroom Fondue

1 cup water
1 ounce dried porcini mushrooms*

2 tablespoons (¼ stick) butter
8 ounces fresh shiitake mushrooms, stemmed, finely chopped
2 tablespoons chopped shallot

1 pound ripe Brie cheese, well chilled, rind trimmed, cheese cut into ½-inch pieces (about 2 cups)
2 tablespoons cornstarch
1 cup dry white wine

Steamed quartered small red-skinned potatoes, steamed asparagus or green beans, and bite-size pieces of French bread or focaccia

Bring 1 cup water to boil in small saucepan. Add porcini mushrooms. Remove from heat and let stand until mushrooms soften, about 20 minutes. Using slotted spoon, transfer porcini to work surface; coarsely chop. Reserve porcini and soaking liquid.

Melt butter in heavy large saucepan over medium heat. Add shiitake mushrooms; sauté until tender, about 3 minutes. Add shallot; sauté 1 minute. Add porcini and soaking liquid, leaving sediment from liquid behind. Increase heat to high. Simmer until liquid evaporates, about 3 minutes. *(Can be made 8 hours ahead. Cover; chill.)*

Toss Brie with cornstarch in large bowl to coat. Add wine to mushrooms. Bring to simmer over medium heat. Add cheese to mushrooms in 3 batches, whisking after each addition until cheese melts before adding more. Whisk until mixture is smooth and just begins to simmer (do not boil). Season with salt and pepper.

Transfer fondue to fondue pot. Set pot over candle or canned heat burner. Serve with vegetables and bread.

**Dried porcini mushrooms are available at Italian markets, specialty foods stores and many supermarkets.*

4 TO 6 SERVINGS

fondue redux

Fondue was big in the sixties and early seventies—now it's back, and better than ever. Dishes known as fondue take their name from the French *fondre,* which means "to melt." Indeed, the two best-known fondues involve melting.

For the classic cheese fondue, Swiss cheeses such as Emmenthal or Gruyère are melted with wine, kirsch and garlic to make a thick mixture into which bite-size chunks of crusty bread are dunked at the ends of long-handled forks. Pieces of vegetable or sausage may also be dipped, and other cheeses and ingredients may be used in the mixture. In Italy, for example, Fontina cheese is combined with milk and egg yolks and topped with shaved white truffle to make *fonduta.*

For dessert fondues, chocolate is melted along with cream and sweet liqueurs. Dipping items may include pound cake, cookies or fresh fruit.

A third type of fondue from France called fondue bourguignonne uses the same heated serving pot as the cheese or chocolate versions. In this case, however, the pot is filled with hot oil in which guests cook bite-size pieces of beef fillet, afterward dipping them into various sauces.

Grilled Blue Cheese Sandwiches with Walnuts and Watercress

1 cup crumbled blue cheese (about 8 ounces)
½ cup finely chopped toasted walnuts
16 slices whole wheat bread, trimmed into crustless 3-inch squares
16 small watercress sprigs

6 tablespoons (¾ stick) butter

Divide cheese and walnuts equally among 8 bread squares. Top each with 2 watercress sprigs. Sprinkle with pepper and top with remaining bread squares, making 8 sandwiches total. Press together gently to adhere. *(Can be made 4 hours ahead. Cover and chill.)*

Melt 3 tablespoons butter in large nonstick griddle or skillet over medium heat. Cook 4 sandwiches on griddle until golden brown and cheese melts, about 3 minutes per side. Transfer to cutting board. Repeat with remaining 3 tablespoons butter and 4 sandwiches.

8 SERVINGS

soup and sandwich supper for eight

Grilled Blue Cheese Sandwiches with Walnuts and Watercress (at right; pictured opposite)

Tossed Green Salad

Beef Barley Soup with Wild Mushrooms and Parsnips (page 49)

Beer or Zinfandel

Black-Bottom Chocolate Pie

Minted Asparagus Frittata

4 large eggs
⅓ cup ricotta cheese
1½ tablespoons chopped fresh mint
¼ teaspoon salt
¼ teaspoon ground black pepper
3 tablespoons grated Parmesan cheese
1 tablespoon olive oil
10 ounces slender asparagus spears, trimmed, cut into ¾-inch pieces
3 green onions, chopped

Preheat broiler. Whisk first 5 ingredients and 2 tablespoons Parmesan in medium bowl to blend. Heat oil in medium nonstick broilerproof skillet over medium heat. Add asparagus and toss to coat. Cover skillet; cook until asparagus is crisp-tender, about 4 minutes. Add onions; stir 30 seconds. Stir in egg mixture. Cover, reduce heat to low and cook until almost set on top, about 8 minutes.

Sprinkle frittata with remaining 1 tablespoon Parmesan. Broil until top is set and starts to brown, about 2 minutes. Slide spatula around frittata to loosen; slide out onto plate and serve.

2 SERVINGS

Double-Crust Leek, Zucchini and Rice Tart

This savory French tart is filled with leeks, zucchini and rice, enriched by Parmesan cheese and a small amount of crème fraîche. It tastes just as good served at room temperature as it does warm from the oven.

CRUST

3 cups all purpose flour
1 teaspoon salt
1 cup (2 sticks) chilled unsalted butter, cut into ½-inch pieces
7 tablespoons (or more) ice water

FILLING

2 tablespoons olive oil
3 large leeks (white and pale green parts only), thinly sliced
4 zucchini (about 22 ounces), diced
½ cup uncooked long-grain white rice
1½ cups water
⅔ cup freshly grated Parmesan cheese
¼ cup crème fraîche or whipping cream
3 large eggs, separated

1 egg, beaten to blend (for glaze)

FOR CRUST: Mix flour and salt in processor. Add butter and cut in using on/off turns until mixture resembles coarse meal. Add 7 tablespoons ice water; process until moist clumps form, adding more water by teaspoonfuls if dough is dry. Gather dough into ball; divide in half. Flatten each half into disk. Wrap each in plastic; chill until firm, about 30 minutes. *(Can be made 1 day ahead. Keep chilled. Let dough soften slightly before rolling out.)*

FOR FILLING: Heat oil in heavy large nonstick skillet over medium heat. Add leeks and sauté until tender, about 8 minutes. Mix in zucchini and rice, then 1½ cups water. Reduce heat to medium-low. Cover and cook until rice is tender and water is absorbed, about 22 minutes. Transfer rice mixture to large bowl and cool completely. Mix in cheese and crème fraîche. Season to taste with salt and pepper. Mix in 3 egg yolks.

Preheat oven to 375°F. Roll out 1 dough disk on lightly floured surface to 13-inch round. Transfer to 11-inch-diameter tart pan with removable bottom. Press dough gently into pan.

Beat 3 egg whites in medium metal bowl to stiff peaks. Fold whites into filling. Spoon filling into crust.

Roll out remaining dough disk on lightly floured surface to 13-inch round. Place dough atop filling. Pinch top and bottom crust edges together to seal. Press dough overhang against top edge of pan to trim excess and form neat edge (discard excess dough). Pierce top crust with fork. Brush with egg glaze.

Bake tart until crust is deep golden, about 1 hour 10 minutes. Cool tart in pan on rack 30 minutes. Remove tart from pan. Serve warm or at room temperature.

6 TO 8 SERVINGS

Wild Mushroom and Blue Cheese Omelets

- 3 tablespoons plus 6 teaspoons butter
- 1 pound assorted wild mushrooms (such as oyster, crimini and stemmed shiitake), chopped
- 1 large onion, finely chopped
- 1 tablespoon dry Sherry
- 3 tablespoons sour cream
- 2 teaspoons minced fresh thyme

- 12 large eggs
- ½ teaspoon salt
- ½ teaspoon ground black pepper

- 1 cup crumbled blue cheese

Melt 3 tablespoons butter in heavy large skillet over high heat. Add mushrooms and onion; sauté until golden brown, about 10 minutes. Mix in Sherry; cook 1 minute. Remove from heat. Mix in sour cream and thyme. Season with salt and pepper. Set aside.

Whisk eggs, salt and pepper in large bowl to blend.

Melt 1 teaspoon butter in 6-inch nonstick skillet over medium-low heat. Pour generous ⅓ cup egg mixture into skillet and cook until almost set, tilting skillet and lifting egg mixture with spatula to allow uncooked portion to run underneath, about 1 minute. Spoon ⅓ cup mushroom mixture over half of omelet. Sprinkle mushrooms with about 2½ tablespoons blue cheese. Cover and cook until cheese melts, about 2 minutes. Fold unfilled half of omelet over filling. Slide omelet out onto plate. Repeat with remaining butter, egg mixture, mushroom filling and cheese, forming total of 6 omelets.

6 SERVINGS

Use any assortment of wild mushrooms you like in these blue cheese-filled omelets. For an attractive garnish, top them with sautéed red bell peppers. Lemon-Pecan Muffins (page 148) make a good accompaniment.

pasta party for six

Endive and Pear Salad with Gorgonzola Cream Dressing (page 138)

Pasta with Roasted Provençal Vegetable Sauce (at right; pictured opposite)

Breadsticks

Pinot Grigio

Peach-Amaretto Sundaes (page 185)

Pasta with Roasted Provençal Vegetable Sauce

- 1 16- to 18-ounce eggplant, unpeeled, cut into 1-inch pieces
- 1 large onion, cut into 1-inch pieces
- 2 tablespoons olive oil
- 2 medium zucchini, trimmed, cut into 1-inch pieces
- 2 garlic cloves, minced
- 1 28-ounce can seasoned crushed tomatoes with Italian herbs

- 12 ounces penne pasta

- ¼ cup chopped fresh parsley
- ¼ cup chopped fresh basil
- 1 tablespoon chopped fresh rosemary
- 1 tablespoon chopped fresh thyme

Preheat oven to 400°F. Arrange eggplant and onion on large rimmed nonstick baking sheet. Drizzle with oil. Sprinkle with salt and pepper. Roast vegetables until beginning to brown, stirring occasionally, about 25 minutes. Stir zucchini and garlic into vegetables; continue to roast until all vegetables are tender, about 20 minutes longer. Stir crushed tomatoes into vegetables on baking sheet; roast until heated through, about 10 minutes.

Meanwhile, cook pasta in large pot of boiling salted water until just tender but still firm to bite, stirring occasionally. Ladle ½ cup pasta cooking liquid into small bowl; reserve. Drain pasta.

Return pasta to same pot. Add roasted vegetable sauce and all herbs to pasta and toss to blend. Gradually add enough reserved pasta cooking liquid to moisten as desired. Season to taste with salt and pepper. Transfer pasta to bowl and serve.

6 SERVINGS

Fettuccine with Prosciutto, Peas and Lemon-Chive Sauce

Fettuccine and peas are tossed with a tart lemon cream sauce flecked with chives in this quick and easy recipe. The Italian ham called prosciutto is cut into slivers and sprinkled over before serving.

- 6 ounces fettuccine
- 1 cup frozen petite peas
- ½ cup whipping cream
- ½ cup chopped fresh chives or green onion tops
- 3 tablespoons fresh lemon juice
- 1½ teaspoons grated lemon peel
- 2 ounces thinly sliced prosciutto, cut into slivers

Cook pasta in large pot of boiling salted water until just tender but still firm to bite. Add peas; cook 30 seconds. Drain, reserving ½ cup pasta cooking water. Return pasta and peas to pot. Add cream, chives, lemon juice and peel to pasta. Toss over medium heat to coat, adding reserved pasta water by tablespoonfuls if dry, about 1 minute. Mix in prosciutto; season with salt and pepper.

2 SERVINGS

Penne with Shrimp, Asparagus and Sun-dried Tomatoes

- ½ cup drained oil-packed sun-dried tomatoes (about 2½ ounces), sliced, 2 tablespoons oil reserved
- 1 pound asparagus, trimmed, cut on diagonal into ½-inch pieces
- 1¼ pounds uncooked shrimp, peeled, deveined
- ½ cup chopped fresh basil
- 2 large garlic cloves, chopped
- ½ teaspoon dried oregano
- ¼ teaspoon dried crushed red pepper
- 1¾ cups canned low-salt chicken broth
- ½ cup dry white wine
- 2 tablespoons tomato paste

- 12 ounces penne pasta
- ¾ cup grated Parmesan cheese

Heat oil reserved from tomatoes in heavy large skillet over medium-high heat. Add asparagus and sauté until crisp-tender, about 5 minutes. Using slotted spoon, transfer asparagus to bowl. Add sun-dried tomatoes, shrimp, ¼ cup basil, garlic, oregano and crushed red pepper to same skillet and sauté until shrimp are just opaque in center, about 3 minutes. Transfer shrimp mixture to bowl with asparagus. Add broth, wine and tomato paste to same skillet. Boil until sauce thickens slightly, stirring occasionally, about 6 minutes.

Cook pasta in large pot of boiling salted water until tender but still firm to bite. Drain; return pasta to same pot. Add shrimp mixture, sauce, remaining ¼ cup basil and cheese to pasta. Toss over medium heat until warmed through and sauce coats pasta. Season with salt and pepper and serve.

4 SERVINGS

Fettuccine Quattro Formaggi

- 1 pound spinach fettuccine

- 1½ cups whipping cream
- ¾ cup crumbled Gorgonzola cheese
- ⅔ cup grated provolone cheese
- ½ cup crumbled soft fresh goat cheese (such as Montrachet)
- ¼ cup (½ stick) butter
- ½ teaspoon dried crushed red pepper
- ¼ teaspoon ground nutmeg

- ¾ cup freshly grated Parmesan cheese
- ¼ cup pine nuts, toasted

This ultra-cheesy cousin of fettuccine Alfredo can be made with any number of four-cheese combinations. Try the varieties included in this recipe, or substitute cheeses like Fontina, Havarti, blue cheese and feta.

Cook spinach fettuccine in large pot of boiling salted water until just tender but still firm to bite.

Combine cream and next 6 ingredients in heavy large saucepan. Whisk over medium heat until mixture simmers and is smooth.

Drain pasta; return to same pot. Add cream sauce and Parmesan to pasta; toss to coat. Season to taste with salt and pepper. Sprinkle with toasted pine nuts and serve.

8 SERVINGS

the greening of america

Strong-tasting leafy greens, usually simmered for hours with smoked pork, were once considered a specialty of the South. Nowadays, cooks everywhere recognize how good greens can be, not just for their pronounced flavor but also for the generous amounts of vitamins A and C, calcium, iron and fiber they provide. Look for the following greens in grocery stores and farmers' markets. (Note that the young, tender leaves may be eaten raw; the larger leaves should be steamed, sautéed or braised.)

- Beet greens: No longer simply discarded from fresh beets, these greens are mild-tasting and tender.
- Collard greens: Rough-edged, these have a mild but distinctive flavor.
- Dandelion greens: These cultivated slender leaves have a tangy flavor with a refreshing edge of bitterness.
- Kale: Crinkly edged kale leaves are gray-green in color with a robust texture and spicy taste.
- Swiss chard: Big beautiful greens, chard has white-to-purple stalks and green leaves. The stalks, which may be cooked separately, taste like celery; the leaves are reminiscent of spinach.
- Turnip greens: These long, notched leaves are slightly sweet when young but develop bite as they mature.

Orecchiette with Greens, Goat Cheese and Raisins

⅓ cup golden raisins
⅓ cup fresh lemon juice

4 tablespoons olive oil
1½ cups finely chopped red onion
3 garlic cloves, minced
1 bunch red or green Swiss chard (about 12 ounces), stems trimmed, leaves coarsely chopped
1 bunch beet greens (about 6 ounces), stems trimmed, leaves coarsely chopped
2 tablespoons minced peeled fresh ginger
1½ tablespoons grated lemon peel

1 pound orecchiette (little ear-shaped pasta)
5 ounces soft fresh goat cheese (such as Montrachet)

Combine raisins and lemon juice in small bowl. Set aside.

Heat 2 tablespoons oil in heavy large pot over medium-low heat. Add onion and sauté until tender, about 8 minutes. Add garlic and sauté until fragrant, about 1 minute. Add Swiss chard, beet greens and raisin mixture. Cover and cook until greens wilt, about 5 minutes. Mix in ginger and lemon peel. Season with salt and pepper.

Meanwhile, cook pasta in large pot of boiling salted water until tender but still firm to bite. Drain. Return pasta to pot. Toss pasta with remaining 2 tablespoons olive oil. Add greens and goat cheese. Toss to combine. Season to taste with salt and pepper. Transfer pasta to large bowl and then serve.

4 TO 6 SERVINGS

Pasta with Tomatoes, Zucchini and Pesto

¼ cup olive oil
4 cups ½-inch cubes zucchini (about 22 ounces)
1½ cups chopped onions
2 large garlic cloves, chopped
1 28-ounce can diced tomatoes in juice

1 pound spaghetti

1 7-ounce package purchased pesto
½ cup thinly sliced fresh basil
Grated Parmesan cheese

Heat oil in heavy large pot over medium-high heat. Add zucchini, onions and garlic and sauté until zucchini is crisp-tender, about 5 minutes. Add tomatoes with juices and simmer until almost all liquid evaporates, about 8 minutes.

Meanwhile, cook pasta in large pot of boiling salted water until just tender but still firm to bite. Drain; return to pot.

Add pesto to pasta and toss to coat. Add zucchini mixture and toss over low heat to combine. Mix in basil. Season with salt and pepper. Transfer pasta to serving bowl. Pass Parmesan separately.

6 SERVINGS

Egg Noodles with Morel Mushrooms and Garbanzo Beans

1 cup canned vegetable broth
¾ ounce dried morel mushrooms

3 tablespoons olive oil
3 large garlic cloves, chopped
1 cup dry white wine
½ cup drained canned garbanzo beans (chickpeas)

8 ounces wide egg noodles, freshly cooked
1 cup grated Parmesan cheese
3 tablespoons chopped fresh thyme

This fast pasta dish gets substance from canned garbanzo beans and morels. Look for dried morel mushrooms in the produce section of the supermarket.

Bring broth and mushrooms to simmer in heavy small saucepan. Remove from heat; let stand until mushrooms soften, about 12 minutes. Using slotted spoon, transfer mushrooms to small bowl; reserve soaking liquid in pan.

Heat oil in heavy large skillet over medium-high heat. Add garlic; stir 30 seconds. Add mushrooms and reserved soaking liquid, leaving any sediment in pan. Add wine and beans. Boil until mushrooms are tender and sauce is reduced by half, about 8 minutes.

Add noodles, ½ cup Parmesan and thyme to sauce. Toss until sauce coats noodles, about 2 minutes. Season with salt and pepper. Serve with remaining ½ cup Parmesan.

2 SERVINGS

Turkey Sausage-Spinach Lasagna with Spicy Tomato Sauce

dinner with the neighbors for ten

Caesar Salad

Turkey Sausage-Spinach Lasagna with Spicy Tomato Sauce (at right; pictured at right)

Garlic Bread with Pecorino Romano Butter (page 149; pictured at right)

Chianti or Zinfandel

Triple-Cherry Cheesecake (page 174)

- 1 tablespoon olive oil
- 1¼ pounds hot Italian turkey sausages, casings removed
- Spicy Tomato Sauce (see recipe opposite)

- 1 15-ounce container ricotta cheese
- 1 10-ounce package frozen chopped spinach, thawed, squeezed dry
- 1¾ cups grated Parmesan cheese
- 2 large eggs
- 3 tablespoons whipping cream
- ½ teaspoon dried basil
- ½ teaspoon dried oregano
- ½ teaspoon ground black pepper

- 9 uncooked lasagna noodles
- 3 cups shredded provolone cheese (about 12 ounces)

Heat oil in large skillet over medium heat. Add sausages; sauté until brown, using fork to break up meat into coarse pieces, about 7 minutes. Add Spicy Tomato Sauce. Simmer 5 minutes.

Position rack in center of oven; preheat to 375°F. Whisk

ricotta, spinach, 1 cup Parmesan, eggs, cream, basil, oregano and pepper in large bowl. Set ricotta mixture aside.

Spoon 1 cup sauce over bottom of 13 x 9 x 2-inch glass baking dish. Place 3 noodles over sauce in single layer. Spread 1 cup sauce over noodles. Spoon 1 cup ricotta mixture over sauce. Sprinkle ¼ cup Parmesan and 1 cup provolone over ricotta mixture. Repeat layering with 3 noodles, 1 cup sauce, 1 cup ricotta mixture, ¼ cup Parmesan and 1 cup provolone. Arrange remaining 3 noodles over cheese. Spoon 1 cup sauce over noodles. Sprinkle remaining ¼ cup Parmesan and 1 cup provolone over lasagna. Dollop remaining ricotta mixture atop lasagna. Spoon 2½ cups sauce around ricotta dollops. Tightly cover baking dish with foil.

Bake lasagna 50 minutes; uncover and continue baking until noodles are tender and lasagna is hot and bubbly, about 25 minutes longer. Let lasagna stand 15 minutes before serving. *(Can be prepared 1 day ahead. Cool slightly. Cover and refrigerate. Rewarm, covered with foil, in 350°F oven about 45 minutes.)*

Meanwhile, rewarm remaining sauce in small saucepan over medium heat. Serve lasagna, passing remaining sauce.

10 SERVINGS

A great thing about this lasagna is that the noodles don't need to be preboiled. The dish has a lot of liquid (in the form of a rich and spicy tomato sauce) and goes into the oven covered, so the noodles cook perfectly as the lasagna bakes.

Spicy Tomato Sauce

- 3 tablespoons olive oil
- 1 medium onion, finely chopped
- 6 garlic cloves, minced
- 1 teaspoon dried oregano
- ¾ teaspoon dried basil
- ¾ teaspoon dried marjoram
- ¾ teaspoon dried crushed red pepper
- 2 28-ounce cans Italian-style tomatoes
- 1 cup canned crushed tomatoes with added puree
- ½ cup dry red wine

Heat oil in heavy large saucepan over medium heat. Add onion, garlic, oregano, basil, marjoram and crushed red pepper. Cover and cook until onion is translucent, stirring occasionally, about 10 minutes. Add remaining ingredients; simmer gently, uncovered, until sauce thickens and measures 8 cups total, breaking up tomatoes with spoon and stirring occasionally, about 1 hour 15 minutes. Season sauce to taste with salt and pepper. *(Can be prepared 2 days ahead. Cool slightly. Cover and refrigerate.)*

MAKES 8 CUPS

Pizza with Caramelized Onions and Gorgonzola Cheese

The red onions and leeks are caramelized by cooking them in a combination of red wine and balsamic vinegar until most of the liquid has evaporated. Purchased crusts make it easy to assemble the pizzas.

3 tablespoons olive oil
5 cups coarsely chopped red onions
4 cups thinly sliced leeks (about 4; white and pale green parts only)
⅔ cup dry red wine
⅓ cup balsamic vinegar
⅓ cup very finely chopped prosciutto (about 2 ounces)
2 tablespoons finely chopped fresh basil
¼ teaspoon cayenne pepper

2 purchased 10-ounce fully baked thin pizza crusts
8 ounces Gorgonzola cheese, crumbled
1 tablespoon minced fresh rosemary

Heat oil in heavy large pot over medium heat. Add onions and leeks and sauté until tender, about 20 minutes. Add wine and vinegar. Cook until most of liquid evaporates and onions are brown, stirring frequently, about 20 minutes longer. Mix in prosciutto, basil and cayenne. Season to taste with salt and black pepper. *(Can be made 2 days ahead. Cover and refrigerate.)*

Preheat oven to 450°F. Place pizza crusts on 2 large baking sheets. Spoon onion mixture evenly atop crusts, leaving 1-inch border around edges. Sprinkle cheese and rosemary over onions.

Bake pizzas until cheese melts and begins to brown and crusts are crisp and golden, about 12 minutes. Cool on baking sheets 5 minutes. Cut pizzas into slices and serve.

MAKES 2 PIZZAS

Flatbread Pizzas with Olives, Feta and Artichokes

2 6-inch-diameter whole wheat pita breads, cut horizontally in half, or one 24 x 9-inch soft Armenian lavash bread, halved crosswise
1 6.5-ounce jar marinated artichoke hearts, drained, marinade reserved, large pieces halved

Either pita bread or Armenian lavash bread, which is often used for sandwich wraps, can serve as the base for these easy-to-make pizzas topped with marinated artichoke hearts, flavored feta cheese and tangy Kalamata olives.

- 1 5-ounce container sun-dried tomato- and basil-flavored feta cheese spread or 1½ cups crumbled flavored feta cheese
- 1 14.5-ounce can diced tomatoes with Italian herbs, drained well
- 1 cup pitted Kalamata olives or other brine-cured black olives, coarsely chopped
- 2 teaspoons dried oregano

Preheat oven to 450°F. Place breads on 2 baking sheets. Brush breads with some of artichoke marinade. Bake until just beginning to color, about 3 minutes. Cool on sheets 5 minutes.

Spread breads almost to edges with feta spread or sprinkle with crumbled feta cheese. Top with tomatoes, olives, oregano and artichokes. Drizzle with remaining artichoke marinade.

Bake pizzas until heated through, 4 minutes. Cut into wedges.

2 SERVINGS

To test whether the dough has risen enough, press two fingers about one inch into it. If the indentations remain, the dough is stretched to its capacity, usually double the initial volume.

As needed, use just a sprinkling of flour on the work surface when rolling out the dough. This keeps the dough from sticking.

Fold the dough over the filling, forming a half circle. To keep the calzone from opening during baking, close the seam by pinching the edges together tightly.

Calzones with Cheese and Sausage

1½ cups warm water (105°F to 115°F)
1 envelope dry yeast
4 tablespoons olive oil
1½ teaspoons salt
4 cups (about) all purpose flour

1 large red bell pepper
1¼ pounds red onions, sliced
4 sweet or spicy Italian sausages, casings removed
3 cups (packed) coarsely grated mozzarella cheese (about 12 ounces)
12 ounces ricotta cheese
4 teaspoons dried oregano

Pour 1½ cups warm water into large bowl. Stir in yeast. Let stand until yeast dissolves, about 5 minutes. Mix in 2 tablespoons oil and salt. Add 3¾ cups flour, about ½ cup at a time, stirring until blended. Turn dough out onto floured surface. Knead until smooth and elastic, sprinkling with more flour if sticky, 10 minutes.

Place dough in oiled large bowl; turn to coat. Cover bowl with plastic wrap. Let rise until doubled, 1 hour 15 minutes.

Meanwhile, char bell pepper over gas flame or in broiler until blackened on all sides. Enclose in paper bag and let stand 10 minutes. Peel, seed and slice pepper. Heat 2 tablespoons olive oil in heavy large skillet over medium-high heat. Add red onions; sauté until brown, about 25 minutes. Set aside. Sauté sausage in heavy medium skillet over medium heat until cooked through, breaking into ½-inch pieces with spoon, about 15 minutes. Set aside. Mix both cheeses and oregano in bowl; season with salt and pepper.

Position 1 rack in top third and 1 rack in bottom third of oven and preheat to 400°F. Dust 2 baking sheets with flour.

Punch dough down. Knead on lightly floured surface until smooth, about 1 minute. Divide into 4 equal portions; shape each into ball. Roll out dough balls on lightly floured surface to 9-inch rounds. Spread ⅓ cup cheese mixture over half of each round, leaving ¾-inch border. Cover cheese on each with ¼ of onions, ⅓ cup cheese mixture, ¼ of sausage, ⅓ cup cheese mixture, then ¼ of bell peppers. Fold plain dough halves over filling, forming half circles. Pinch edges of dough firmly together to seal.

Using spatula, transfer 2 calzones to each sheet. Pierce tops in several places. Bake calzones 15 minutes. Reverse baking sheets; bake until tops are golden brown, about 15 minutes.

MAKES 4

This page: Roasted Herb Potato Medley (page 122). Opposite, top: Hot and Smoky Baked Beans (page 124). Opposite, bottom: Tomato, Cucumber and Red Onion Salad with Mint (page 137).

on the side

Roasted Herb Potato Medley

- ½ cup olive oil
- ½ cup balsamic vinegar
- ¼ cup chopped shallots
- 5 teaspoons chopped fresh thyme or 2 teaspoons dried
- 5 teaspoons chopped fresh rosemary or 2 teaspoons dried
- 2 teaspoons fennel seeds, chopped
- 3 pounds medium-size red-skinned potatoes, each cut into 8 wedges
- 3 pounds medium-size Yukon Gold potatoes, each cut into 8 wedges

Fresh thyme and rosemary sprigs

Preheat oven to 400°F. Oil 2 large baking sheets. Whisk first 6 ingredients in large bowl. Add potatoes. Sprinkle with salt and pepper. Toss to coat. Using slotted spoon, transfer potatoes to sheets, spreading in single layer. Reserve oil mixture in bowl.

Roast potatoes until tender and golden, stirring and turning potatoes occasionally, about 1 hour. Return potatoes to reserved oil mixture in bowl; toss. Garnish with herb sprigs.

10 SERVINGS

Orzo Pilaf with Green Onions and Parmesan Cheese

The rice-shaped pasta orzo is sometimes labeled *riso* or *rosamarina*. Here it is cooked in chicken broth, with green onions and Parmesan cheese mixed in at the end.

- 3¼ cups (or more) canned low-salt chicken broth
- 1 pound orzo (rice-shaped pasta)
- 5 green onions, thinly sliced
- ¾ cup grated Parmesan cheese

Bring 3¼ cups broth to boil in heavy large saucepan over medium-high heat. Mix in orzo and simmer uncovered until just tender but still firm to bite and some broth still remains, stirring occasionally, about 8 minutes. Remove from heat. Add green onions and cheese and stir to blend. Season pilaf to taste with salt and pepper. Rewarm over low heat, if necessary, and mix in more broth by ¼ cupfuls if pilaf is dry. Transfer pilaf to large bowl and serve.

6 SERVINGS

Marinated Tempeh Stir-fry with Broccoli and Red Bell Pepper

- 4 ounces soy tempeh or 3-grain tempeh, cut into ½-inch pieces
- ¼ cup light soy sauce
- 1 tablespoon rice vinegar
- 3 garlic cloves, minced
- 2 teaspoons minced peeled fresh ginger
- ⅛ teaspoon dried crushed red pepper

- 12 ounces broccoli, stems peeled and cut into ½-inch pieces, florets cut into 1-inch pieces
- 2 tablespoons water
- 1 teaspoon honey
- 1 teaspoon cornstarch
- 1 tablespoon vegetable oil
- ½ cup chopped red bell pepper
- 2 tablespoons thinly sliced green onion

Stir tempeh, soy, vinegar, garlic, ginger and crushed red pepper in medium bowl to blend. Marinate 1 hour at room temperature.

Steam broccoli until crisp-tender, about 3 minutes. Set aside. Strain marinade from tempeh into small bowl; set tempeh aside. Whisk 2 tablespoons water, honey and cornstarch into marinade.

Heat oil in large nonstick skillet over high heat. Add marinated tempeh and bell pepper and sauté 4 minutes. Add broccoli and marinade mixture; sauté until broccoli is heated through and sauce thickens, 3 minutes. Transfer to bowl. Sprinkle with green onion.

4 SERVINGS

soy to the world

A staple in Asia for thousands of years, soybeans have gradually found their way into mainstream Western cooking. Enjoyed simply as cooked beans, either dried or in the fresh green form known by the Japanese as *edamame*, soybeans also give us such products as custard-textured bean curd or tofu; solid, chewy tempeh, a meat substitute made from soybeans and grains; soy milk, a low-fat milk substitute; and miso, a rich-tasting fermented soybean paste used as a seasoning or condiment. (Look for these at natural foods stores.)

Apart from their versatility, soy products are also winning converts with the outstanding health benefits they offer. They are excellent sources of protein and fiber, along with B vitamins and minerals. Their fat content is mostly unsaturated. And perhaps best of all, soy is an excellent source of isoflavones, a type of plant hormone that researchers now believe may help decrease the risk of various forms of cancer, lower blood levels of the "bad" LDL cholesterol, help keep bones healthy and diminish the symptoms of menopause. Try the tempeh stir-fry at left; it's a great way to add soy to your diet.

Hot and Smoky Baked Beans

Canned *chipotle* chilies give the beans a kick, while bacon provides a smoky flavor. Serve the baked beans either hot from the oven or at room temperature.

- 6 bacon slices
- 1½ cups chopped onions
- 1¼ cups purchased barbecue sauce
- ¾ cup dark beer
- ¼ cup mild-flavored (light) molasses
- 3 tablespoons Dijon mustard
- 3 tablespoons (packed) dark brown sugar
- 2 tablespoons Worcestershire sauce
- 1 tablespoon soy sauce
- 4 to 6 teaspoons minced canned chipotle chilies*
- 6 15- to 16-ounce cans Great Northern beans, drained
- Chopped fresh parsley

Preheat oven to 350°F. Cook bacon in large skillet over medium heat until crisp. Transfer to paper towels and drain. Transfer 2½ tablespoons bacon drippings from skillet to large bowl. Finely chop bacon; add to bowl. Add onion and next 7 ingredients to bowl and whisk to blend. Whisk in 4 to 6 teaspoons chipotle chilies, depending on spiciness desired. Stir in beans.

Transfer bean mixture to 13 x 9 x 2-inch glass baking dish. Bake uncovered until liquid bubbles and thickens slightly, about 1 hour. Cool baked beans 10 minutes. Sprinkle with parsley and serve.

*Chipotle *chilies canned in a spicy tomato sauce, sometimes called* adobo, *are available at Latin American markets, specialty foods stores and some supermarkets.*

8 TO 10 SERVINGS

Dill Mashed Potatoes with Crème Fraîche and Caviar

3½ pounds russet potatoes, peeled, cut into 2-inch pieces
1 cup crème fraîche or sour cream
¼ cup (½ stick) butter, room temperature
3 tablespoons (packed) finely chopped fresh dill

1 4-ounce jar salmon caviar

Crème fraîche and caviar make these potatoes extra rich and utterly delicious. If you can't find crème fraîche at the market, sour cream is a fine substitute.

Cook potatoes in large pot of boiling salted water until very tender, about 25 minutes. Drain well. Return potatoes to pot; mash over low heat until almost smooth. Add crème fraîche and butter; whisk until smooth and fluffy. Stir in dill. Season with salt and pepper. *(Potatoes can be made 2 hours ahead. Cover and let stand at room temperature. Rewarm over low heat, stirring frequently.)*

Top mashed potatoes with caviar and serve.

6 TO 8 SERVINGS

Thyme-roasted Potatoes with Balsamic Vinegar

2 pounds small red-skinned potatoes, scrubbed, halved
Olive oil-flavored nonstick vegetable oil spray
4 tablespoons chopped fresh thyme
2 teaspoons garlic salt

1½ cups white* or regular balsamic vinegar
3 tablespoons sugar

Preheat oven to 400°F. Place potatoes in large bowl. Generously spray potatoes with nonstick spray. Toss to coat. Sprinkle with 3 tablespoons thyme and garlic salt. Toss to coat. Spray large rimmed baking sheet with nonstick spray. Arrange potatoes, cut side down, on sheet. Roast potatoes until tender and golden brown, turning every 15 minutes and roasting about 45 minutes total.

Meanwhile, stir vinegar and sugar in heavy small saucepan over high heat until sugar dissolves. Boil until liquid is reduced to ⅔ cup, about 10 minutes. Mix in remaining 1 tablespoon thyme.

Drizzle some balsamic syrup over potatoes and serve.

**White balsamic vinegar is available at many supermarkets.*

6 SERVINGS

Bell Pepper and Eggplant Tian

Before peeling the bell peppers, enclose them in a paper bag for ten minutes—the steam inside loosens their skin and makes them much easier to peel.

Layer half of the eggplant, garlic, thyme, olives, tomatoes, anchovies and bell peppers in the baking dish. Then repeat the layering, starting with the eggplant.

4 large red bell peppers (about 2 pounds)

9 tablespoons olive oil
2 1-pound eggplants, peeled, cut crosswise into ¼- to ½-inch-thick rounds

3 cups fresh breadcrumbs made from crustless French bread

3 garlic cloves, minced
3 tablespoons chopped fresh thyme
7 tablespoons coarsely chopped pitted Niçois olives
6 large plum tomatoes, thinly sliced
1 2-ounce can anchovy fillets, drained

Roast red bell peppers directly over gas flame or in broiler until blackened on all sides. Enclose in paper bag and let stand 10 minutes. Peel and seed peppers; cut into scant ½-inch-wide strips.

Preheat oven to 450°F. Brush each of 2 large baking sheets with 1 tablespoon oil. Arrange eggplant rounds in single layer on baking sheets; sprinkle eggplant rounds on each baking sheet with 1 tablespoon olive oil. Bake until eggplant begins to soften but not brown, 15 minutes. Remove from oven; maintain oven temperature.

Heat 1 tablespoon oil in heavy large skillet over medium heat. Add breadcrumbs and sauté until golden, about 6 minutes.

Arrange half of eggplant in single layer in 12 x 9 x 2-inch oval baking dish. Sprinkle eggplant rounds with half of garlic, 1 tablespoon thyme and 3 tablespoons olives. Top with half each of tomatoes, anchovy fillets and pepper strips, spacing evenly. Sprinkle lightly with salt and generously with pepper. Drizzle with 2 tablespoons oil. Repeat layering with remaining eggplant rounds, garlic, 1 tablespoon thyme and 3 tablespoons olives. Top with remaining tomatoes, spacing evenly, leaving 1½-inch-wide space at edge of baking dish. Arrange remaining bell peppers and anchovies between tomato slices. Drizzle with remaining 2 tablespoons oil. Sprinkle with 1 tablespoon chopped olives.

Bake tian 30 minutes. Sprinkle breadcrumbs and remaining 1 tablespoon thyme around edge of baking dish. Continue to bake tian until vegetables are very tender, about 15 minutes. Let stand 15 minutes. Serve tian hot or at room temperature.

8 SERVINGS

Risotto-Style Barley with Spring Greens

In this recipe, barley is cooked as you would rice for a risotto—slowly, simmering until the broth is absorbed and then adding more. The result is a rich-tasting side dish that is actually low in fat and cholesterol.

- Nonstick vegetable oil spray
- 2 large leeks (white and pale green parts only), chopped
- 1 fennel bulb, finely chopped (about 1½ cups)
- 1 teaspoon dried thyme
- 2 cups pearl barley
- 6½ cups canned low-salt chicken broth
- ½ teaspoon saffron threads

- 1½ cups frozen baby lima beans, thawed

- 1 6-ounce package fresh baby spinach, trimmed, thinly sliced
- ¼ cup grated Parmesan cheese
- 2 tablespoons chopped fresh basil
- Fresh basil sprigs

Generously spray heavy large pot with nonstick spray. Place pot over medium-high heat. Add half of leeks and half of fennel to pot. Sauté until vegetables are tender, about 5 minutes. Stir in thyme, then barley. Add 2½ cups broth and saffron. Simmer until liquid is almost absorbed, stirring frequently, about 10 minutes. Add remaining leeks, fennel and 4 cups broth. Bring to simmer. Reduce heat to medium-low and cook until barley is tender and mixture is creamy, stirring often, about 30 minutes.

Meanwhile, cook lima beans in large saucepan of boiling salted water until tender but still bright green, 3 minutes. Drain.

Add lima beans, spinach, Parmesan cheese and chopped basil to barley and stir to blend. Season with salt and pepper. Transfer mixture to 6 shallow bowls. Garnish with basil sprigs and serve.

6 SERVINGS

Saffron-Cardamom Rice

- 3 teaspoons butter
- ¼ cup pine nuts
- ½ cup chopped red onion
- 1 cup basmati rice*
- 1½ cups water
- 2 tablespoons golden raisins
- 1 teaspoon sugar
- ¾ teaspoon salt
- ¼ teaspoon crumbled saffron threads
- ¼ teaspoon ground cardamom

Melt 1 teaspoon butter in small skillet over medium heat. Add pine nuts; sauté until golden, about 5 minutes. Cool.

Melt remaining 2 teaspoons butter in medium saucepan over medium heat. Add onion and sauté until slightly softened, about 5 minutes. Add rice and stir 2 minutes. Add 1½ cups water, raisins, sugar, salt, saffron and cardamom. Bring to boil. Reduce heat, cover and simmer until rice is tender, about 15 minutes. Remove from heat; let stand covered 10 minutes. Stir in pine nuts.

**Available at Indian markets and some supermarkets.*

4 SERVINGS

Spicy Rice and Kale

- 2¼ cups canned low-salt chicken broth or vegetable broth
- 1½ teaspoons Creole or Cajun seasoning
- 1 cup converted white rice
- 4 ounces kale (about ½ large bunch), stems and ribs removed, leaves coarsely chopped (2 cups packed)

Bring broth and Creole seasoning to boil in heavy large saucepan. Stir in rice and kale; bring to boil. Reduce heat to low, cover and cook until rice is tender and liquid is absorbed, about 20 minutes.

4 SERVINGS

the cardamom of india

With its almost balsamic muskiness, evocative of aniseed and pepper, cardamom is an essential spice in many different cuisines. West Indian curry is defined by its presence. Throughout India, the spice is an integral component of the spice blend *garam masala.* In Sweden, it flavors pastries and meatballs alike. It scents *pfeffernusse* cookies in Germany, liqueurs in Russia, and coffee among the Bedouins of North Africa.

Traditionally cardamom, a relative of ginger, has come from India. Since the 1980s, however, Guatemala has led the world in its cultivation, in 1997 exporting more than 60 times what India did.

Whatever the source, you will find the spice as seeds in a pod, as whole seeds out of the pod, or as ground seeds. Use a rolling pin to crush whole pods in a plastic bag. The seeds can then be crushed in a mortar with a pestle or ground in a coffee grinder. Or leave cardamom whole: Two or three pods can infuse a pan of rice with delicate flavor. Ground cardamom scents the rice dish at top left.

Broccoli Rabe with Garlic and Pecorino Romano Cheese

2 pounds broccoli rabe,* tough stems peeled

¼ cup extra-virgin olive oil
5 garlic cloves, coarsely chopped
6 tablespoons freshly grated pecorino Romano cheese

Cook broccoli rabe in large pot of boiling salted water until crisp-tender, about 2 minutes. Drain and transfer to bowl of ice water to cool. Drain again; pat dry. *(Can be made 1 day ahead. Wrap in paper towels. Enclose in plastic bag and chill.)*

Heat olive oil in heavy large skillet over medium heat. Add garlic and sauté until fragrant, about 1 minute. Add broccoli rabe and sauté until heated through, about 4 minutes. Remove from heat. Sprinkle 4 tablespoons cheese over and toss to combine. Season broccoli rabe with salt and pepper. Transfer to warm platter. Sprinkle remaining 2 tablespoons cheese over and serve.

**Broccoli rabe, also known as* rapini, *is a type of leafy green stalk with scattered clusters of small broccoli-like florets; available at many specialty foods stores and some supermarkets.*

6 SERVINGS

Ratatouille

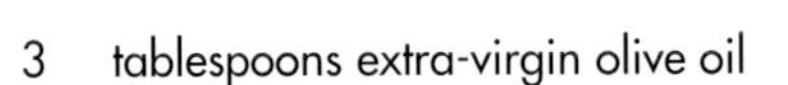

3 tablespoons extra-virgin olive oil
2 cups chopped onions
2 1-pound eggplants, unpeeled, cut into 1-inch cubes
4 garlic cloves, minced
2 zucchini, cut into 1-inch pieces
1 red bell pepper, cut into 1-inch pieces
1 yellow bell pepper, cut into 1-inch pieces
2¾ pounds ripe tomatoes, seeded, coarsely chopped (about 6 cups)
3 fresh thyme sprigs
1 fresh rosemary sprig
1 bay leaf
¼ cup minced fresh basil

Heat oil in heavy large pot over medium heat. Add onions and sauté until tender, about 10 minutes. Add eggplants and garlic; sauté

5 minutes. Add zucchini and bell peppers; sauté 5 minutes. Mix in tomatoes, thyme, rosemary and bay leaf. Reduce heat to medium-low. Cover and cook until vegetables are tender and flavors have blended, stirring occasionally, about 40 minutes. Discard bay leaf; stir in basil. Season ratatouille generously with salt and pepper. Transfer to bowl. *(Can be prepared 8 hours ahead. Cover and refrigerate.)* Serve ratatouille cold, warm or hot.

8 SERVINGS

Mashed Potatoes with Pancetta and Leeks

- 12 ounces Yukon Gold potatoes (about 2 medium), unpeeled
- 2 ounces sliced pancetta* or 3 bacon slices, chopped
- 3 tablespoons extra-virgin olive oil
- 2 cups chopped leeks (white and pale green parts only)
- ¾ teaspoon dried thyme
- ¼ cup ¼-inch peeled carrot pieces
- ⅓ cup ¼-inch zucchini pieces

Cook unpeeled potatoes in medium pot of boiling salted water until tender, approximately 30 minutes.

Meanwhile, sauté sliced pancetta in large skillet over medium heat until crisp, 10 minutes. Transfer pancetta to small bowl. Add 1 tablespoon olive oil to same skillet. Reduce heat to medium-low. Add leeks and thyme; sauté until leeks are tender, about 5 minutes. Add carrot pieces; sauté 4 minutes. Add zucchini pieces; sauté until vegetables are crisp-tender, about 1 minute longer.

Drain potatoes. Peel and return to same pot. Add remaining 2 tablespoons oil and mash to chunky puree. Stir in pancetta and vegetable mixture. Season with salt and pepper. *(Can be made 2 hours ahead. Let stand at room temperature. Rewarm over low heat.)*

**Available at Italian markets and some supermarkets.*

2 SERVINGS

the potato mash

Who would have thought that plain old mashed potatoes would generate such excitement among food lovers today? Look at the menu of any fashionable restaurant, though, and you're likely to see some version of the homely pureed spuds, gussied up with roasted garlic, other root vegetables, various cheeses, or all kinds of other ingredients (such as the version at left with pancetta and leeks).

Cooks, too, are giving serious thought to the best way to prepare the potatoes themselves. For the best texture, follow these kitchen-tested guidelines:

- Precook: Slice the potatoes and precook them well below a simmer for 20 to 30 minutes. This causes starch to swell in the potatoes' granules.
- Cool: Let the potatoes cool in their water. This allows the starch to firm up.
- Cook: Boil the potatoes until tender. Drain well; return to pan and heat them briefly to dry them out.
- Mash gently: Pass the potatoes through a ricer or push them through a large-holed strainer. (Old-fashioned mashers are okay to use, too, though they release more starch.)
- Enrich and season: Stir in butter, hot milk or cream, and salt and pepper to taste. Serve immediately.

Green Bean Salad with Apricot Vinaigrette

- 1 11½-ounce can apricot-pineapple nectar
- ¼ cup rice vinegar
- ¼ cup chopped dried apricots (about 1 ounce)

- 1¼ pounds slender green beans, trimmed

- 1 5-ounce package mixed baby greens

- 1 papaya, peeled, seeded, thinly sliced lengthwise
- 3 tablespoons chopped unsalted dry roasted pistachios
- 1½ ounces ricotta salata* or feta cheese, crumbled

There is not a drop of oil in this unique salad, which makes it low in fat. The dressing is a pureed mix of apricot-pineapple nectar, reduced until thickened; rice vinegar; and sweet dried apricots.

Boil nectar in medium saucepan until reduced to scant ⅔ cup, about 5 minutes. Mix in vinegar and apricots. Let stand until apricots soften, about 15 minutes. Puree mixture in blender. Season to taste with salt and pepper. Cool.

Cook green beans in large pot of boiling salted water until crisp-tender, about 5 minutes. Drain. Cool in large bowl of ice water. Drain again. Pat beans dry with paper towels. *(Can be prepared 1 day ahead. Wrap green beans in paper towels. Cover vinaigrette and green beans separately and refrigerate.)*

Place beans in large bowl. Add 6 tablespoons vinaigrette and toss to coat. Season with salt and pepper. In another large bowl, toss mixed greens with enough remaining vinaigrette to coat. Season to taste with salt and pepper.

Mound mixed greens in center of 6 plates. Surround with papaya slices. Arrange beans atop mixed greens. Sprinkle with pistachios and ricotta salata.

**Ricotta salata is available at cheese shops, some Italian markets and some specialty foods stores.*

6 SERVINGS

blood oranges of the mediterranean

Until recently, it was rare to find blood oranges in American markets. Only within the past decade have they appeared in grocery stores from December to May. With a less acidic taste than standard oranges and virtually seed-free flesh ranging from solid garnet to ruby striations, blood oranges are a delight.

They are believed to have come from a spontaneous mutation of standard oranges, probably in Sicily in the seventeenth century. For the best color to develop, the fruit needs mild, sunny days and crisp nights. Today, the finest are still grown in Sicily, where the climate promotes brilliant coloration, but blood oranges are also cultivated elsewhere in Italy as well as in Spain, Morocco and Malta. The most common varieties found in American markets are the round Moro and the oval Tarocco, both with a slight raspberry flavor; and the larger Sanguinelli, which tastes of strawberries.

Spring Greens with Roasted Beets and Blood Oranges

4 medium beets, trimmed

3 tablespoons olive oil
2 tablespoons Sherry wine vinegar or balsamic vinegar
1½ tablespoons walnut oil or olive oil
8 cups mixed baby greens
2 blood oranges, peel and white pith removed, oranges thinly sliced
½ cup finely chopped red onion
¼ cup walnuts, toasted, chopped

Preheat oven to 450°F. Wrap beets in foil, enclosing completely. Roast until tender when pierced with skewer, about 1 hour 15 minutes. Cool. Peel beets and cut into ½-inch pieces.

Whisk olive oil, vinegar and walnut oil in small bowl to blend. Season to taste with salt and pepper. Place mixed baby greens in large bowl. Arrange blood orange slices, red onion and beets atop. Drizzle dressing over salad. Sprinkle with toasted walnuts; serve.

4 SERVINGS

Roasted Potato Salad with Sage

6 tablespoons extra-virgin olive oil
3 tablespoons red wine vinegar
3 tablespoons minced shallots

3½ pounds small red-skinned potatoes (about 50)
35 fresh sage leaves, trimmed

Whisk 3 tablespoons oil, vinegar and shallots in medium bowl to blend. Season vinaigrette with salt and pepper.

Preheat oven to 425°F. Toss potatoes, sage and remaining 3 tablespoons oil in large roasting pan to coat. Sprinkle with salt and pepper. Roast until potatoes are tender and sage is crisp, stirring occasionally, about 45 minutes. Cool slightly.

Cut potatoes in half. Transfer to large bowl. Crumble roasted sage leaves over. Rewhisk vinaigrette; drizzle over. Toss to coat. Season with salt and pepper. Serve warm or at room temperature.

10 SERVINGS

Tomato, Cucumber and Red Onion Salad with Mint

- 2 large English hothouse cucumbers, halved lengthwise, seeded
- ⅓ cup red wine vinegar
- 1 tablespoon sugar
- 1 teaspoon salt

- 3 large tomatoes, seeded, coarsely chopped
- ⅔ cup coarsely chopped red onion
- ½ cup chopped fresh mint
- 3 tablespoons olive oil

Cut cucumber halves diagonally into ½-inch-wide pieces. Place in large bowl. Add vinegar, sugar and salt. Let stand at room temperature 1 hour; toss occasionally.

Add tomatoes, red onion, mint and oil to cucumbers and toss to blend. Season salad with salt and pepper.

6 SERVINGS

A colorful salad of tomatoes, cucumbers, red onion and mint is easy to make and goes well with a variety of warm-weather dishes.

You can make the noodle salad and the dressing a day ahead and store them separately; then toss them together right before serving. Look for tahini at Middle Eastern markets and natural foods stores; *soba* can be found at Asian markets.

Spicy Sesame and Ginger Noodle Salad

- ¾ cup low-sodium soy sauce
- 9 tablespoons fresh lemon juice
- 6 tablespoons minced peeled fresh ginger
- 6 tablespoons tahini (sesame seed paste)
- 4½ tablespoons honey
- 2 teaspoons dried crushed red pepper
- 6 tablespoons oriental sesame oil

- 3 8-ounce packages chuka soba (thin yellow Japanese noodles)
- 6 medium carrots, peeled, cut into matchstick-size strips
- 1½ cucumbers, peeled, seeded, cut into matchstick-size strips
- 1½ bunches green onions, thinly sliced diagonally
- 12 ounces snow peas, trimmed, thinly sliced diagonally
- 3 red bell peppers, cut into matchstick-size strips
- ¼ cup sesame seeds, toasted

Whisk first 6 ingredients in medium bowl to blend. Mix in 3 tablespoons oriental sesame oil.

Cook noodles in large pot of boiling salted water until just tender but still firm to bite, stirring occasionally, about 5 minutes. Drain. Transfer hot noodles to large bowl. Toss with remaining 3 tablespoons oil. Add all vegetables; toss well. *(Salad and dressing can be made 1 day ahead. Chill separately.)* Toss with dressing; season with salt and pepper. Sprinkle with sesame seeds and serve.

14 SERVINGS

Endive and Pear Salad with Gorgonzola Cream Dressing

- 4 tablespoons apple cider vinegar
- 3 tablespoons olive oil
- 1 tablespoon honey
- 4 large heads Belgian endive, sliced
- 1 large pear, halved, cored, sliced
- ⅓ cup sour cream
- ⅓ cup plain yogurt
- 1¼ cups crumbled Gorgonzola cheese

½ cup hazelnuts, toasted, husked
Chopped fresh chives

Whisk 3 tablespoons vinegar, oil and honey in large bowl to blend. Add endive and pear and toss to coat. Blend sour cream, yogurt and remaining 1 tablespoon vinegar in medium bowl; mix in cheese. Season dressing to taste with salt and pepper. Mound salad on platter. Top with dressing, nuts and chives.

6 SERVINGS

Confetti Salad with Ranch Dressing

1 English hothouse cucumber, chopped
1 16-ounce bag frozen petite peas, thawed
2 bunches radishes, chopped
1 cup chopped celery
½ cup finely chopped red onion
Ranch Dressing (see recipe below)

Combine all vegetables in large bowl. *(Can be prepared 4 hours ahead. Cover and refrigerate.)* Toss salad with enough Ranch Dressing to coat. Season to taste with salt and pepper and serve.

6 SERVINGS

Ranch Dressing

¾ cup mayonnaise
½ cup buttermilk
2 tablespoons powdered cultured buttermilk blend*
2 tablespoons finely chopped fresh parsley
2 tablespoons finely chopped celery leaves
1½ teaspoons fresh lemon juice
1½ teaspoons Dijon mustard
¾ teaspoon onion powder
¼ teaspoon dried dillweed

Whisk first 3 ingredients in large bowl. Mix in remaining ingredients. Cover and chill at least 1 hour to blend flavors. *(Dressing can be prepared 5 days ahead. Keep refrigerated.)*

**Powdered cultured buttermilk blend is available alongside the canned and powdered milk in most supermarkets.*

MAKES 1½ CUPS

what's in a name?

Wondering where the unusual name of your favorite salad dressing comes from? Look no further.

- Caesar: Italian restaurateur Caesar Cardini threw together this blend of olive oil, garlic, coddled eggs, Parmesan, mustard, lemon juice and Worcestershire sauce in Tijuana in 1924.
- Green Goddess: Flecked with fresh herbs and green onion, this mayonnaise dressing was invented in San Francisco in the mid 1920s to honor actor George Arliss, starring in William Archer's play *The Green Goddess.*
- Ranch: A buttermilk mixture seasoned with garlic, lemon or lime juice and herbs, this dressing was devised in the 1950s at the Hidden Valley Guest Ranch in Santa Barbara, California.
- Russian: An American-born dressing first mentioned in print about 1922, this mayonnaise-based mixture with bell pepper, chives and pimientos may get its name from the red hue of chili sauce or ketchup, or from the fact that some early versions contained caviar.
- Thousand Island: Perhaps whimsically named for the many bits of minced pickled cucumber in it or for the thousand islands in the St. Lawrence River where it may have originated, this is a version of Russian dressing.

Green Salad with Goat Cheese, Artichoke Hearts and Croutons

Homemade croutons sautéed with prosciutto, garlic and oregano add crunch and flavor to this elegant salad.

4 6.5-ounce jars marinated artichoke hearts, well drained
12 tablespoons extra-virgin olive oil
4 garlic cloves, minced
3 tablespoons minced fresh oregano
6 ounces thinly sliced prosciutto, coarsely chopped (about 1½ cups)
5 cups ½-inch pieces crustless baguette (from one 16-ounce loaf)
6 cups lightly packed bite-size pieces romaine lettuce
4 cups lightly packed arugula (about 2 large bunches)
⅔ cup sliced red onion
4 tablespoons Sherry wine vinegar or balsamic vinegar
1½ cups crumbled soft fresh goat cheese (about 5 ounces)

Combine artichoke hearts, 6 tablespoons oil, 2 minced garlic cloves and 1 tablespoon oregano in medium bowl. Refrigerate at least 2 hours and up to 6 hours, tossing occasionally.

Heat remaining 6 tablespoons oil in heavy large skillet over medium-high heat. Add prosciutto; stir 2 minutes. Add bread pieces; stir to coat with oil. Mix in remaining 2 garlic cloves and 2 tablespoons oregano. Reduce heat to medium-low; stir until bread pieces begin to brown and are crisp on edges, about 10 minutes.

Place romaine, arugula, red onion and vinegar in large bowl. Add artichoke mixture; toss to blend. Season with salt and pepper. Spoon bread mixture over. Sprinkle with goat cheese.

10 SERVINGS

Arugula, Fennel and Orange Salad

- ¼ cup minced shallots
- 3 tablespoons extra-virgin olive oil
- 1½ tablespoons fresh lemon juice
- 2 large oranges
- 7 cups arugula (about 10 large bunches), trimmed
- 1 large fennel bulb, quartered lengthwise, cored, thinly sliced crosswise
- 1 small red onion, thinly sliced

Whisk minced shallots, olive oil and lemon juice in medium bowl to blend. Season dressing to taste with salt and pepper.

Cut all peel and white pith from oranges. Using small sharp knife, cut between membranes to release segments. Combine arugula, fennel and onion in large bowl. Toss with enough dressing to coat. Add orange segments; toss. Season with salt and pepper.

6 SERVINGS

Artichoke, Lima and Pea Salad

- ¼ cup red wine vinegar
- 2 tablespoons minced shallot
- 2 tablespoons whipping cream
- ¼ cup extra-virgin olive oil
- 2 14½-ounce cans chicken broth
- 1 16-ounce bag frozen baby lima beans
- 2 14-ounce cans water-packed artichoke hearts, drained, quartered
- 1 16-ounce bag frozen petite peas
- ¼ cup chopped fresh mint
- Fresh mint sprigs

Whisk vinegar, shallot and cream in small bowl. Gradually whisk in oil. Season vinaigrette with salt and pepper.

Bring chicken broth to simmer in large saucepan. Add lima beans. Cover and simmer until tender, about 10 minutes. Using slotted spoon, transfer beans to large bowl. Add artichoke hearts to broth. Cook 2 minutes. Add peas. Cover and cook until peas and artichokes are heated through, about 3 minutes longer. Drain well. Add to beans.

Add chopped mint to vegetables. Mix in enough vinaigrette to coat. Season with salt and pepper. Garnish with mint sprigs.

10 SERVINGS

the fennel family

Looking remarkably like a squashed or stunted head of celery, the bulb vegetable called fennel—in fact, a variety known as Florence fennel—is prized foremost for its crisp texture and its refreshing anise taste. The bulb can be eaten raw when sliced as a salad ingredient, as in the recipe at left. It can also be cooked by sautéing, grilling, braising or roasting, and goes especially well with seafood dishes.

The feathery fronds of the fennel bulb should not be discarded. They can be used as a fresh herb, either chopped in salads or as a seasoning for cooked fish. In fact, another type of the bulb—common fennel—is specifically grown for its fronds. If either Florence or common fennel is allowed to grow to maturity, the plants ultimately produce crescent-shaped, sweet, anise-flavored fennel seeds, which are commonly sold as a commercial seasoning. The seeds are used to enhance liqueurs, as well as both sweet and savory dishes.

Modern Macaroni Salad

2⅓ cups elbow macaroni (about 10 ounces)

⅔ cup mayonnaise
¼ cup Dijon mustard
2 tablespoons fresh lemon juice
1½ tablespoons sugar
1⅓ cups chopped drained bread-and-butter pickles
1¼ cups chopped celery
2 4-ounce jars sliced pimientos, drained
½ cup thinly sliced green onions

Cook macaroni in large pot of boiling salted water just until tender but still firm to bite, stirring occasionally. Drain. Rinse under cold water; drain macaroni thoroughly.

Whisk mayonnaise, mustard, lemon juice and sugar in large bowl. Mix in macaroni, pickles, celery, pimientos and green onions. Season to taste with salt and pepper.

6 TO 8 SERVINGS

lakeside lunch for six

Deviled Eggs with Curry
(page 12)

The Best BLTs
(page 65)

Modern Macaroni Salad
(at left; pictured opposite)

Celery Sticks, Carrot Sticks and Olives

Iced Tea

Cherry-Berry Lattice Pie
(page 156)

Grilled Squash Salad with Basil-Parmesan Dressing

4 medium-large zucchini, trimmed, halved lengthwise
4 medium-large yellow crookneck squash, trimmed, halved lengthwise
5 tablespoons olive oil

½ cup chopped fresh basil
⅓ cup freshly grated Parmesan cheese (about 1 ounce)
2 tablespoons balsamic vinegar

Prepare barbecue (medium heat). Place zucchini and crookneck squash on large baking sheet; brush all over with 3 tablespoons oil. Sprinkle with salt and pepper. Grill vegetables until tender and brown, turning occasionally, 10 minutes. Transfer to plate; cool.

Cut vegetables diagonally into 1-inch-wide pieces. Place in large bowl. Add basil, Parmesan cheese, balsamic vinegar and remaining 2 tablespoons oil; toss to blend. Season with salt and pepper; serve.

6 SERVINGS

Three-Pepper Slaw with Chili Dressing

❖

Here's a unique no-cabbage slaw (bell peppers and jicama are the stand-ins) with a dressing that is both spicy (*chipotle* chilies) and a little sweet (a touch of honey).

- 5 tablespoons fresh lemon juice
- 3 tablespoons fat-free mayonnaise
- 2 tablespoons honey
- 5 garlic cloves
- 2 teaspoons minced canned chipotle chilies*
- 1½ teaspoons chili powder

- 1 large red bell pepper, cut into thin strips
- 1 large green bell pepper, cut into thin strips
- 1 large yellow bell pepper, cut into thin strips
- 12 ounces jicama, peeled, cut into thin strips

- ⅓ cup chopped fresh Italian parsley

Puree first 6 ingredients in blender. Season to taste with salt and pepper. *(Can be made 1 day ahead. Cover and refrigerate.)*

Toss bell peppers, jicama and dressing in large bowl to coat. Season slaw with salt. Cover and refrigerate until vegetables soften slightly but are still crunchy, about 4 hours.

Mix chopped parsley into slaw. Serve at room temperature.

*Chipotle *chilies canned in a spicy tomato sauce, sometimes called* adobo, *are available at Latin American markets, specialty foods stores and some supermarkets.*

8 SERVINGS

Red Potato Salad with Onions and Olives

- 5½ pounds red-skinned potatoes, cut into ¾-inch pieces
- 1¼ cups dry white wine

- 6 tablespoons red wine vinegar
- 4 teaspoons Dijon mustard
- 3 garlic cloves, minced
- 1¼ cups olive oil
- 2 red bell peppers, halved, seeded, cut into thin strips
- 12 green onions, chopped
- 1 large red onion, thinly sliced

- 1¼ cups Kalamata olives or other brine-cured black olives, pitted, halved lengthwise
- ¾ cup (packed) chopped drained oil-packed sun-dried tomatoes
- 1 cup chopped fresh parsley

Steam potatoes in batches until tender, about 8 minutes per batch. Transfer hot potatoes to large bowl. Pour wine over; toss to combine. Cool to lukewarm.

Mix vinegar, mustard and garlic in small bowl. Gradually whisk in oil. Pour over potatoes. Mix in bell peppers, green onions, red onion, olives and tomatoes. Season with salt and pepper. Let stand 1 hour to allow flavors to blend. *(Can be prepared 1 day ahead. Cover and chill.)* Add parsley to salad; toss to combine.

12 SERVINGS

Green Bean and Shiitake Mushroom Salad

This appealing side-dish salad is ideal for entertaining since the beans can be cooked a day ahead and the entire salad can be assembled and left at room temperature up to two hours before serving.

- 3 pounds green beans, trimmed

- ¼ cup plus ⅔ cup olive oil
- 12 ounces fresh shiitake mushrooms, stemmed, sliced
- 2 teaspoons chopped fresh thyme
- ½ cup chopped shallots

- ¼ cup balsamic vinegar
- 2 teaspoons Dijon mustard

Cook beans in large pot of boiling salted water until crisp-tender, about 5 minutes. Drain. Transfer to bowl of ice water; cool. Drain well. Pat dry with paper towels. *(Can be made 1 day ahead. Cover with plastic wrap and refrigerate.)*

Heat ¼ cup oil in heavy large skillet over medium heat. Add mushrooms and thyme; sauté until mushrooms are brown, 5 minutes. Add shallots; sauté 2 minutes. Season with salt and pepper.

Whisk vinegar and mustard in large bowl. Gradually whisk in ⅔ cup oil. Add beans and mushrooms; toss to coat. Season salad to taste with salt and pepper. *(Can be prepared up to 2 hours ahead. Let stand at room temperature.)*

12 SERVINGS

Ciabatta

Refrigerating the firm starter dough, called a *biga*, overnight transforms it into a loose, spongy mass. Pulling the biga into pieces the next day makes it easier to mix with the other ingredients.

Unlike standard bread doughs, during the initial mixing stage *ciabatta* dough is very soft, almost like cooked oatmeal. Mixing it in a bowl keeps the dough contained.

BIGA

1 cup plus 1 tablespoon room-temperature water (75°F to 80°F)
1 ¼-ounce package dry yeast
3⅓ cups bread flour

DOUGH

¾ cup plus 2 tablespoons room-temperature water (75°F to 80°F)
Pinch of dry yeast
½ cup plus 3 tablespoons semolina flour*

2½ teaspoons salt

Additional semolina flour

FOR BIGA: Place water in processor. Sprinkle yeast over. Let stand until yeast dissolves, about 8 minutes. Add 1 cup flour; process until blended. Scrape down sides of work bowl. Add 1 cup flour; repeat processing and scraping. Add remaining 1⅓ cups flour. Process until small moist clumps form. Gather dough into ball (dough will be firm); place in large bowl. Cover; chill overnight (biga will soften, resembling thick oatmeal in texture).

FOR DOUGH: Pull biga into walnut-size pieces; place in a clean large bowl. Add ¾ cup plus 2 tablespoons water, yeast and ½ cup plus 3 tablespoons semolina. Using 1 hand, squeeze ingredients together 2 minutes. Work dough 4 minutes by scooping sections from sides of bowl and pressing into center, blending into very soft, shaggy mass. Using spatula, scrape dough from sides of bowl into center. Let dough rest in bowl, uncovered, 10 minutes.

Sprinkle 2½ teaspoons salt over dough. Using 1 hand, knead dough by rotating bowl ¼ turn at a time, scooping dough from sides and folding down into center until dough starts to come away from sides of bowl, about 5 minutes. Scrape dough from hand and sides of bowl. Cover bowl with towel; let dough rest 20 minutes.

Rotating bowl ¼ turn at a time, fold soft dough over onto itself

6 times, then turn dough over in bowl. Cover with clean towel and let dough rest in bowl 20 minutes.

Preheat oven to 425°F. Sprinkle work surface with additional semolina flour. Turn dough out onto semolina. Using pastry scraper or large knife, cut dough in half; keep halves separated. Let dough halves stand, uncovered, 20 minutes.

Sprinkle 2 large baking sheets with additional semolina. Transfer each dough half, semolina side up, to 1 sheet. Stretch each dough half to 16 x 4-inch rectangle. Press fingertips into dough in several places to dimple surface (characteristic of this bread). Bake until golden brown, about 25 minutes. Cool. *(Can be prepared 2 weeks ahead. Double-wrap in aluminum foil to freeze.)*

**Also called pasta flour, semolina flour is available at natural foods stores, Italian markets and some supermarkets.*

MAKES 2 LOAVES

During the second mixing stage, the dough is still soft but less sticky. Because it has developed some gluten, which lends elasticity, it will start to pull away from the sides of the mixing bowl.

Since the dough remains soft throughout, shape it right on the baking sheet; pull the dough into the traditional long loaf. Semolina keeps the dough from sticking.

Lemon-Pecan Muffins

❖

These moist muffins practically melt in your mouth. Studded with toasted chopped pecans, they get an extra hit of fresh flavor from grated lemon peel.

2 cups all purpose flour
⅔ cup sugar
4 teaspoons grated lemon peel
1 tablespoon baking powder
½ teaspoon salt
¼ teaspoon baking soda
½ cup (1 stick) chilled unsalted butter, cut into pieces
¾ cup sour cream
2 large eggs
½ cup pecans, toasted, chopped

Preheat oven to 400°F. Line ten ⅓-cup muffin cups with paper liners. Mix first 6 ingredients in medium bowl to blend. Cut in chilled butter until mixture forms coarse crumbs. Mix in sour cream and eggs. Mix in chopped pecans.

Divide batter among prepared cups. Bake until tester inserted into center of muffins comes out clean and tops are golden brown, about 25 minutes. Turn out onto rack and cool.

MAKES 10

Bacon and Thyme Biscuits

4 bacon slices, chopped

2⅓ cups all purpose flour
4 teaspoons baking powder
1 tablespoon sugar
1 teaspoon dried thyme
¾ teaspoon salt
½ teaspoon baking soda
½ cup chilled solid vegetable shortening, cut into pieces
¾ cup buttermilk

Melted butter

Preheat oven to 400°F. Cook bacon in heavy large skillet over medium heat until crisp, about 4 minutes. Using slotted spoon, transfer bacon to paper towels; drain. Reserve 2 tablespoons drippings.

Mix flour, baking powder, sugar, dried thyme, salt and baking soda in large bowl. Add chilled shortening; cut in until mixture resembles coarse meal. Add buttermilk, reserved bacon drippings and chopped bacon; stir until mixture is just combined. Gather dough together. Turn dough out onto lightly floured surface; knead several turns until smooth. Pat out dough to 8-inch round. Cut into 8 wedges. Transfer wedges to baking sheet, spacing 2 inches apart.

Bake biscuits until puffed and golden, about 18 minutes. Brush tops with butter. *(Can be made 1 day ahead. Cool completely. Wrap in foil; let stand at room temperature. Rewarm in 350°F oven until heated through, about 5 minutes.)* Serve warm.

MAKES 8

Garlic Bread with Pecorino Romano Butter

- ½ cup (1 stick) unsalted butter, room temperature
- ½ cup grated pecorino Romano cheese
- ¼ cup finely chopped fresh Italian parsley
- 2 garlic cloves, minced

- 1 14-inch-long loaf Italian or French bread, halved lengthwise

Mix butter, cheese, parsley and garlic in medium bowl to blend well. Season with pepper. *(Can be prepared 1 day ahead. Cover and refrigerate. Bring to room temperature before using.)*

Preheat oven to 500°F. Place bread, cut side up, on baking sheet. Spread butter mixture evenly over cut sides of bread. Bake until topping is golden brown and bread is heated through, about 5 minutes.

Cut bread crosswise into 2-inch-wide pieces. Serve immediately.

10 SERVINGS

There's no need for store-bought garlic bread when you can make this delicious version in minutes. The butter-garlic mixture can be prepared up to a day ahead.

Fougasse with Provençal Herbs

- 1½ cups warm water (105°F to 115°F)
- 1 teaspoon dry yeast
- 4 cups (about) unbleached all purpose flour
- 2 tablespoons dried herbes de Provence*
- 2 teaspoons fine sea salt
- 4 tablespoons olive oil

Yellow cornmeal

Fougasse is a distinctive oval flatbread from Provence with a leaf-like motif. A mix of dried herbs typical of the region and a drizzle of olive oil are all that's needed to season the bread before baking.

Pour 1½ cups warm water into large bowl; sprinkle yeast over. Let stand until yeast dissolves, about 10 minutes. Stir in 1 cup flour, 1 tablespoon herbes de Provence and sea salt, then 2 tablespoons oil until well blended. Mix in enough flour, 1 cup at a time, to form thick and slightly sticky dough.

Turn dough out onto lightly floured work surface; knead until smooth and elastic, about 5 minutes. Form into ball. Oil large bowl. Add dough; turn to coat. Cover bowl with plastic wrap, then towel. Let rise in warm draft-free area until doubled, about 1 hour.

Position 1 rack in center and 1 rack in top third of oven and preheat to 450°F. Sprinkle 2 baking sheets generously with cornmeal. Punch dough down. Turn out onto floured surface; divide in half. Press out each half to 11 x 8-inch irregularly shaped oval. Transfer to prepared baking sheets. Brush each oval with 1 tablespoon oil. Sprinkle each with 1½ teaspoons herbes de Provence. Using sharp knife, make several 2-inch-long cuts in each oval (do not cut

through edges), spacing cuts evenly apart and cutting through dough to work surface. Pull dough apart at cuts to create openings. Cover loosely with plastic; let rise in warm draft-free area until slightly puffed, about 20 minutes.

Place dough in oven. Immediately pour about ¼ cup water onto bottom of oven, creating steam. Bake breads until golden on top and slightly crisp on bottom, switching sheets between racks and turning front of each sheet to back of oven halfway through baking, about 18 minutes. Transfer sheets to racks; cool breads 10 minutes. Serve warm or at room temperature.

**A dried herb mixture available at specialty foods stores and in the spice section of some supermarkets. A combination of dried thyme, basil, savory and fennel seeds can be substituted.*

MAKES 2 LOAVES

Chipotle Corn Bread

- 1 cup yellow cornmeal
- 1 cup all purpose flour
- ¼ cup sugar
- 2 teaspoons baking powder
- 1 teaspoon baking soda
- 1 teaspoon salt
- 1 cup grated Monterey Jack cheese
- 1 cup buttermilk
- 3 large eggs
- 6 tablespoons (¾ stick) unsalted butter, melted, cooled
- 2 tablespoons minced seeded canned chipotle chilies*

Preheat oven to 375°F. Butter 9 x 5 x 2½-inch metal loaf pan. Mix first 6 ingredients in large bowl. Stir in cheese. Whisk buttermilk, eggs, melted butter and chipotles in medium bowl. Add buttermilk mixture to dry ingredients; stir until blended. Spoon batter into prepared pan. Bake bread until tester inserted into center comes out clean, about 35 minutes. Cool in pan on rack 15 minutes. Turn bread out onto rack; cool completely.

*Chipotle *chilies canned in a spicy tomato sauce, sometimes called* adobo, *are available at Latin American markets, specialty foods stores and some supermarkets.*

MAKES 1 LOAF

Not your run-of-the-mill corn bread, this delicious, moist version includes spicy canned *chipotle* chilies and Monterey Jack cheese. It's great with chili.

desserts

Opposite: Poached Pears with Sweet Wine and Fruit Confetti (page 167). Left: Peach-Amaretto Sundaes (page 185). Above: Flourless Chocolate Cake with Chocolate Glaze (page 168).

fig facts

Small enough to be consumed in a bite or two, pear-shaped, plump and juicy figs are (so archaeologists and biblical scholars tell us) among the oldest fruits on the planet. Certainly their succulent texture and honeyed taste offer one of nature's most primal pleasures.

You can find figs in well-stocked markets throughout the year, but summer sees the fruit at its best. Look for any of the three varieties: the pink-fleshed, dark purple-skinned Black Mission; the green-skinned, pale-fleshed Calimyrna; and the small, yellow-green, purple-fleshed Kadota. Choose unblemished specimens that feel full and heavy. Enjoy them fresh on their own or accompanied by thinly sliced prosciutto; or cook them with pork. For dessert, simmer them in sweetened red wine or bake them under a pastry crust or crumb topping.

Dried figs, most often produced from the Calimyrna and Black Mission varieties, are readily available year-round. Eat them as is, use them whole in compotes, or chop and add them to fruit cakes or pies, like the homespun pear and fig pie at right.

Pear and Fig Pie

CRUST

½ cup hazelnuts (about 2 ounces), toasted, husked, cooled
4½ teaspoons sugar
½ teaspoon salt
2½ cups unbleached all purpose flour
¾ cup (1½ sticks) chilled unsalted butter, cut into ¼-inch pieces
6 tablespoons (about) ice water

FILLING

1 cup dried figs (about 7 ounces), stemmed, quartered
½ cup sugar
2 tablespoons unbleached all purpose flour
1 tablespoon fresh lemon juice
1 teaspoon grated lemon peel
2¼ pounds pears, peeled, quartered, cored, thinly sliced

FOR CRUST: Finely grind nuts, sugar and salt in processor. Blend in flour. Add butter and cut in using on/off turns until butter is in rice-size pieces. Blend in 4 tablespoons ice water, adding more water by tablespoonfuls until dough comes together in moist clumps. Gather dough into ball. Divide in half; flatten into disks. Wrap each in plastic; refrigerate until cold, about 45 minutes. *(Can be made 1 day ahead. Keep refrigerated. Let dough soften slightly at room temperature before rolling out.)*

FOR FILLING: Preheat oven to 400°F. Combine first 5 ingredients in large bowl. Add pears and toss to blend.

Roll out 1 dough disk on lightly floured surface to 12-inch round. Transfer to 9-inch-diameter glass pie dish; fill with pear mixture. Roll out second dough disk on lightly floured surface to 12-inch round; place atop filling. Trim overhang of top and bottom crusts to ½ inch; press together and fold under. Crimp edge decoratively. Cut several slits in top crust to allow steam to escape.

Bake pie 20 minutes. Reduce oven temperature to 350°F. Bake pie until juices bubble thickly through vents and crust is golden, about 50 minutes longer. Cool pie on rack 45 minutes. Serve warm or at room temperature.

8 SERVINGS

Cherry-Berry Lattice Pie

This luscious pie is brimming with fresh cherries and blackberries. Use a cherry pitter to remove the pits (the easiest way) before cutting the cherries in half.

CRUST

2 cups all purpose flour
5 tablespoons sugar
½ teaspoon salt
¾ cup (1½ sticks) chilled unsalted butter, cut into ½-inch pieces
1 large egg
2 tablespoons (or more) milk

FILLING

4 cups fresh cherries (about 1½ pounds), pitted, halved
2 cups fresh blackberries or boysenberries, or frozen, thawed, drained
¾ cup sugar
2 tablespoons quick-cooking tapioca
2 teaspoons fresh lemon juice
¼ teaspoon vanilla extract

2 tablespoons (¼ stick) unsalted butter
Sugar

FOR CRUST: Blend flour, sugar and salt in processor. Add butter. Using on/off turns, process until mixture resembles very coarse meal. Beat egg with 2 tablespoons milk; add to processor. Blend until moist clumps form, adding more milk by tablespoonfuls if dough is dry. Gather dough into ball; divide into 2 pieces, 1 slightly larger than the other. Flatten each piece into disk and wrap in plastic; refrigerate 1 hour. *(Can be made 1 day ahead. Keep refrigerated. Let soften slightly at room temperature before rolling out.)*

FOR FILLING: Toss first 6 ingredients in large bowl to blend. Let stand until tapioca is translucent, tossing occasionally, 35 minutes.

Preheat oven to 400°F. Roll out larger dough disk on floured surface to 13-inch round; transfer to 9-inch-diameter deep-dish glass pie dish with 1¾-inch-high sides. Spoon in filling; dot with butter. Roll out remaining dough disk to 7 x 11-inch rectangle. Cut lengthwise into 10 generous ½-inch-wide strips (reserve remaining dough for another use). Arrange 5 strips across pie. Arrange 5 strips diagonally across first strips. Cut overhang of bottom crust and strips to ¾ inch. Fold under; crimp edge. Sprinkle lattice with sugar.

Place pie on baking sheet; bake 30 minutes. Cover edge with foil. Continue to bake until filling bubbles thickly, about 50 minutes longer. Cool 45 minutes. Serve warm or at room temperature.

8 SERVINGS

Walnut Tartlets

Pastry Crust Dough (6 dough disks; see recipe below)
- 1 cup whipping cream
- ½ cup sugar
- ¼ cup (packed) golden brown sugar
- ¼ cup honey
- 1 teaspoon grated orange peel
- ½ teaspoon whole aniseed
- 1¾ cups walnuts, toasted, chopped

These rustic tartlets are chock-full of chopped toasted walnuts. Scented with honey, orange and aniseed, they can be served warm or at room temperature.

Preheat oven to 400°F. Roll out 1 pastry disk on floured surface to 6-inch round. Transfer to 4½-inch-diameter tartlet pan with removable bottom. Press crust onto bottom and up sides of pan; trim overhang to ½ inch. Fold overhang in and press, forming double-thick sides. Repeat with remaining dough disks and 5 more pans. Chill crusts while making filling.

Stir cream and next 5 ingredients in heavy medium saucepan over medium-low heat until sugar dissolves. Increase heat; boil until mixture bubbles thickly and color darkens slightly, about 6 minutes. Remove from heat; stir in walnuts.

Place crusts on baking sheet. Divide filling among crusts. Bake tartlets until filling bubbles thickly and crusts are golden, about 25 minutes. Cool tartlets in pans on rack 5 minutes. Remove pan sides while tartlets are warm. Serve warm or at room temperature.

6 SERVINGS

Pastry Crust Dough

- 2 cups unbleached all purpose flour
- ⅓ cup sugar
- 1 teaspoon salt
- ½ teaspoon grated orange peel
- 1 cup (2 sticks) chilled unsalted butter, cut into ½-inch pieces
- 3 large egg yolks, beaten to blend

Mix first 4 ingredients in large bowl. Add butter; rub in with fingertips until mixture resembles coarse meal. Add yolks; mix with fork until dough begins to clump together. Shape dough into 6 balls. Flatten balls into disks; wrap in plastic. Chill 30 minutes. *(Can be made 2 days ahead. Keep chilled. Let dough soften slightly at room temperature before rolling out.)*

MAKES 6 CRUSTS

all-american peanut butter

Open any cupboard in the country and you're likely to find it: peanut butter, the American pantry staple that's a favorite with kids and adults alike. Whether it's extra-chunky or smooth, that jar of peanut butter likely got its start with the same production process.

Most commercial peanut butters are made with the Runner peanut, a variety common in the South. Once harvested, dried and shelled, the nuts are transported to factories around the country for roasting, skinning and grinding.

"Old-fashioned" or "natural" peanut butters then go to the market. Others undergo a second production phase, whereby salt and sweeteners are added; stabilizers—partially hydrogenated oils—are usually added too, to keep the peanut oil from separating. If cholesterol buildup associated with these trans fatty acids is a concern, seek "old-fashioned" brands, which don't have the stabilizers.

Different recipes may call for different types of peanut butter: creamy varieties for smoothness; crunchy, with bits of chopped peanut mixed in, for texture; natural for its lack of seasonings; stabilized for uniform consistency. For best results, use the type specified.

Peanut Butter and White Chocolate Cream Pie

1 cup sifted powdered sugar
¾ cup smooth old-fashioned peanut butter
2½ teaspoons vanilla extract
2 tablespoons Grape-Nuts cereal

2½ cups whole milk
4 large egg yolks
¾ cup sugar
¼ cup all purpose flour
¼ cup cornstarch
6 ounces good-quality white chocolate (such as Lindt or Baker's), chopped

1 9-inch-diameter frozen pie shell, baked according to package directions, cooled completely
2 ripe bananas, peeled, sliced
1½ cups chilled whipping cream, beaten to firm peaks

Using fork, mix powdered sugar, peanut butter and 1 teaspoon vanilla extract in medium bowl until mixture resembles coarse dry crumbs. Place Grape-Nuts cereal in small bowl. Mix ½ cup peanut butter mixture into cereal; set aside.

Whisk ¼ cup milk, yolks, sugar, flour and cornstarch in bowl to blend. Pour remaining 2¼ cups milk into heavy medium saucepan; bring to simmer. Gradually whisk hot milk into yolk mixture. Return mixture to saucepan. Whisk constantly over medium heat until custard boils and thickens, about 2 minutes. Remove from heat. Add white chocolate and remaining 1½ teaspoons vanilla; whisk until chocolate melts. Cool custard completely.

Sprinkle ½ cup plain (no cereal) peanut butter mixture over bottom of pie shell. Spoon half of custard filling over. Top with bananas, then remaining plain peanut butter mixture. Spoon remaining custard filling over, mounding in center. Refrigerate pie until cold, about 3 hours. *(Can be made 6 hours ahead. Keep chilled.)* Top with whipped cream and sprinkle with peanut butter-cereal mixture. Cut into wedges and serve.

8 SERVINGS

Apricot-Almond Tarts

This recipe yields two apricot tarts, which makes it a great dessert to serve at a party. Almonds used in both the crust and the filling are a nice complement to the apricots.

CRUST

- 2 cups all purpose flour
- ¾ cup almonds, toasted, cooled
- ½ cup sugar
- ¾ teaspoon salt
- 1 cup (2 sticks) chilled unsalted butter, cut into small pieces
- 2 tablespoons (or more) ice water
- 1 large egg yolk
- 1 teaspoon almond extract

FILLING

- 1 cup apricot preserves

- 1½ cups almonds, toasted, cooled
- 1½ cups sugar
- ½ teaspoon ground cinnamon
- 18 (about) large apricots, halved, pitted

FOR CRUST: Blend flour, almonds, sugar and salt in processor until nuts are finely chopped. Add butter; cut in using on/off turns until mixture resembles fine meal. Add 2 tablespoons water, yolk and extract. Blend until moist clumps form, adding more water by teaspoonfuls if dough is dry. Gather dough into ball. Divide into 2 equal pieces. Press each piece onto bottom and up sides of 9-inch-diameter tart pan with removable bottom. Chill 30 minutes. *(Can be prepared 1 day ahead. Cover; keep chilled.)*

FOR FILLING: Set rack at lowest position in oven and preheat to 375°F. Place large sheet of foil on bottom of oven to catch any juices. Stir preserves in small saucepan over low heat until melted; strain preserves into another saucepan.

Finely grind almonds, 1 cup sugar and cinnamon in processor. Spoon over bottom of crusts. Arrange apricot halves, rounded side up, in crusts, fitting snugly together. Brush apricots in each tart with 2 tablespoons preserves. Sprinkle ¼ cup sugar over each tart.

Bake until apricots are tender, 1 hour. Cool tarts 1 hour.

Stir remaining apricot preserves in saucepan over low heat until warm, then brush ¼ cup over each tart.

Remove pan sides from tarts. *(Tarts can be made 8 hours ahead. Let stand at room temperature.)*

MAKES 2 TARTS

Spiced Peach Pie with Buttermilk Crust

Process the dough just until the butter and lard or shortening are reduced to pea-size pieces. The bits of fat will separate the crust into flaky layers while it bakes.

To keep the dough from breaking or tearing, roll it loosely over the rolling pin to transfer it from the work surface to the pie. The pin also makes it easier to center the dough over the fruit filling.

CRUST

2½ cups all purpose flour
5 teaspoons sugar
½ teaspoon salt
6 tablespoons chilled unsalted butter, cut into ½-inch pieces
¼ cup frozen lard or solid vegetable shortening, cut into ½-inch pieces
¾ cup plus 2 tablespoons (about) chilled buttermilk

FILLING

¾ cup plus 1 tablespoon sugar
¼ cup all purpose flour
1½ teaspoons fresh lemon juice
½ teaspoon ground cinnamon
¼ teaspoon ground cardamom
3¾ to 4 pounds ripe peaches
2 tablespoons (¼ stick) unsalted butter, cut into small pieces
1 egg, beaten to blend (for glaze)

FOR CRUST: Blend flour, sugar and salt in processor. Add butter and lard; cut in using on/off turns until fat is reduced to pea-size pieces, about 25 turns. Using on/off turns, blend in ¾ cup buttermilk until dough just comes together in moist clumps, adding more buttermilk if dough is dry. Gather dough into ball. Divide into 2 pieces, 1 slightly larger than the other. Flatten each into disk. Wrap disks in plastic; chill at least 1 hour or overnight.

FOR FILLING: Mix ¾ cup sugar and next 4 ingredients in large bowl. Cook peaches in pot of boiling water 30 seconds. Transfer to bowl of cold water; cool. Peel, halve and pit peaches. Slice peaches into bowl with sugar mixture; toss to coat. Let filling stand until juices form, stirring often, about 20 minutes.

Place 1 rack in center and 1 rack at lowest position in oven; preheat to 400°F. Roll out larger dough disk on floured surface to 12- to 13-inch round. Transfer dough to 9-inch-diameter glass pie dish. Trim overhang to ¾ inch. Mound filling in dish; dot with

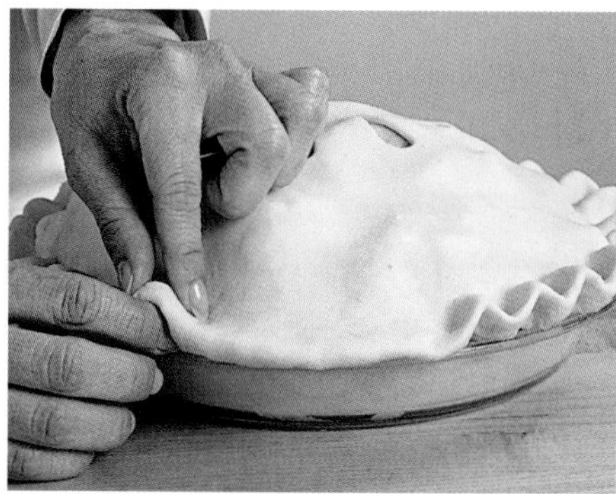

Form a decorative edge on the pie by pressing the dough between the index finger of one hand and the index finger and thumb of the other hand. Repeat the process until the entire edge is fluted.

butter. Roll out second disk on floured surface to 12-inch round. Gently roll up dough onto rolling pin; drape dough over filling. Pinch overhang and edge of top crust together. Fold edge under. Cut several slits in top crust. Crimp edge. Brush pie with beaten egg; sprinkle with remaining 1 tablespoon sugar.

Place pie on center rack in oven. Bake 50 minutes. Place baking sheet on lowest rack to catch drippings. Continue to bake pie until crust is brown and juices bubble thickly through slits, covering very loosely with foil if top browns too quickly, about 20 minutes. Cool on rack 1 hour. Serve warm or at room temperature.

8 SERVINGS

cooking with flowers

Some of spring and summer's prettiest blossoms can add color and flavor to sweet and savory dishes alike. Most traditionally, flowers are used in the form of "waters" such as rose water and orange flower water, sweet essences that add heady perfume to pastries, confections and fruits, like the colorful melange at right. Dried or candied flowers, especially violets, lavender and roses, are popular garnishes for desserts.

Fresh flowers, too, may be employed to striking effect in everything from salads to syrups, flavored butters to cake decorations. When using them, choose only those that you know without question to be edible. Also, make sure that they were not treated with potentially harmful fertilizers or pesticides. Buy only from a source that produces them specifically for the table; or grow them yourself.

Try the following fresh blooms:

- Honeysuckle: Small, slender, sweetly fragrant orange or yellow flowers.
- Lavender: Richly perfumed, sweet-tasting purple blossoms.
- Nasturtiums: Trumpet-shaped, yellow to bright orange flowers tasting pleasantly peppery.
- Pansies: Dainty sweet blossoms ranging from violet to orange.
- Roses: Delicately aromatic petals in a wide range of hues.

Fresh Fruit with Rose Water Syrup

1½ cups water
½ cup sugar
1 cinnamon stick, broken in half
1 teaspoon rose water*

4 oranges
2 cups red grapes, halved
1 1-pint basket strawberries, halved
1 pear, cored, sliced

Stir 1½ cups water and sugar in heavy medium saucepan over medium-low heat until sugar dissolves. Increase heat to medium-high. Add cinnamon; boil until syrup is reduced to scant 1 cup, about 10 minutes. Mix in rose water; cool.

Using small sharp knife, cut off peel and white pith from oranges. Working over large bowl, cut between membranes to release segments into bowl. Add grapes, berries and pear; toss to combine. Mix in syrup. *(Can be made 2 hours ahead. Cover; chill.)*

Spoon fruit and syrup into 6 bowls and serve.

**Rose water is available at Middle Eastern markets and also at some specialty foods stores.*

6 SERVINGS

Pear and Maple Crumble

Served with sour cream, this homespun dessert is a delicious combination of pears and raisins, which are tossed with maple syrup and accented with chopped crystallized ginger. The fruit is baked under a topping made sweet from brown sugar and crunchy from walnuts.

TOPPING

- 1 cup all purpose flour
- 1 cup walnuts
- ⅔ cup (packed) golden brown sugar
- ½ cup (1 stick) chilled unsalted butter, cut into small pieces

PEARS

- 3½ pounds firm but ripe Anjou pears, peeled, cored, cut into ½-inch pieces
- ⅔ cup pure maple syrup
- ½ cup raisins
- 2 tablespoons all purpose flour
- 2 tablespoons fresh lemon juice
- 1 tablespoon finely chopped crystallized ginger
- Sour cream

FOR TOPPING: Combine all ingredients in processor. Process until nuts are coarsely chopped. Cover; chill until firm, 1 hour.

FOR PEARS: Position rack in center of oven and preheat to 350°F. Toss all ingredients except sour cream in large bowl to blend. Let pear mixture stand 15 minutes.

Transfer pear mixture to 13 x 9 x 2-inch baking dish. Sprinkle topping over pears. Bake until juices bubble thickly, about 30 minutes. Let stand 10 minutes. Serve warm with sour cream.

6 TO 8 SERVINGS

Tropical Fruit Compote with Mango Sorbet

- ¾ cup water
- ½ cup dry white wine
- ½ cup sugar

- ½ pineapple, peeled, cored, cut into ¾-inch pieces (about 2 cups)
- 3 kiwis, peeled, halved crosswise, each half quartered
- 1 mango, peeled, pitted, cut into ¾-inch pieces
- 1½ tablespoons fresh lime juice
- 1 teaspoon grated lime peel

- 1½ pints mango sorbet

Combine ¾ cup water, wine and sugar in small saucepan. Bring to boil, stirring until sugar dissolves. Chill syrup until cold.

Combine pineapple, kiwis, mango, lime juice, lime peel and chilled syrup in large bowl. Mix well. Cover fruit mixture and refrigerate for at least 1 hour or overnight.

Scoop ½ cup mango sorbet into each of 6 compote dishes or wineglasses. Spoon fruit mixture around sorbet.

6 SERVINGS

Strawberries in Red Wine

- 3 16-ounce baskets strawberries, hulled, halved
- 1 750-ml bottle of dry red wine
- ¾ cup sugar

Place berries in large bowl. Add wine and sugar; stir gently. Cover; chill 3 to 6 hours. Ladle mixture into wineglasses.

12 SERVINGS

Fresh cranberries are usually sold only from November through January. So buy a few extra bags when you can and freeze them to make this any time of the year.

❖

Cranberry-Apple Crisp

TOPPING

- 1 cup unbleached all purpose flour
- ¾ cup old-fashioned oats
- ⅔ cup (packed) golden brown sugar
- 1 teaspoon ground cinnamon
- ¼ teaspoon salt
- ½ cup (1 stick) chilled unsalted butter, cut into small pieces

FRUIT

- 2 pounds Granny Smith apples, peeled, quartered, cored, thinly sliced
- 2 cups cranberries (about 8 ounces)
- ⅓ cup pure maple syrup
- 2 tablespoons (packed) golden brown sugar
- 1 tablespoon unbleached all purpose flour
- 1 teaspoon grated lemon peel
- Chilled whipped cream

FOR TOPPING: Mix flour, oats, sugar, cinnamon and salt in medium bowl. Rub in butter with fingertips until moist clumps form. *(Can be prepared 1 day ahead. Cover and refrigerate.)*

FOR FRUIT: Preheat oven to 375°F. Butter 11 x 8 x 2-inch ovenproof dish (or another shallow 8-cup-capacity dish). Mix apples and next 5 ingredients in large bowl. Transfer to dish. Bake 20 minutes. Remove from oven. Crumble topping over. Bake until juices bubble thickly around sides, about 35 minutes. Let stand at least 10 minutes and up to 1 hour. Serve with whipped cream.

6 SERVINGS

Poached Pears with Sweet Wine and Fruit Confetti

In this elegant dessert, kiwi, cantaloupe and strawberries are chopped and used as the "confetti" garnish for pears poached in wine, pear nectar, cinnamon and vanilla.

- 6 small firm but ripe Anjou pears, peeled
- 3½ cups sweet white or red wine (such as Moscato) from 1-liter bottle
- 2 cups pear nectar
- 1 cinnamon stick, broken in half
- 1 vanilla bean, split lengthwise

- 1½ teaspoons arrowroot

- ½ cup chopped peeled kiwi
- ½ cup chopped peeled seeded cantaloupe
- ½ cup quartered hulled strawberries
- Fresh mint sprigs

Using melon baller, remove core from bottom end of pears. Combine wine, pear nectar and cinnamon stick in large pot. Scrape in seeds from vanilla bean; add bean. Bring to simmer. Add pears (liquid should cover pears halfway). Reduce heat to medium-low; cook until pears are tender, about 10 minutes, turning pears halfway through. Transfer pears and cooking liquid to large bowl. Cool.

Drain poaching liquid back into pot. Mix 2 tablespoons liquid with arrowroot in small bowl; return to pot. Boil until sauce thickens and is reduced to 2 cups, stirring occasionally, about 12 minutes. Cool sauce to room temperature. *(Pears and sauce can be prepared 1 day ahead. Cover separately and refrigerate. Bring to room temperature before serving.)*

Spoon sauce into 6 shallow bowls. Place pears atop sauce. Sprinkle kiwi, cantaloupe and strawberries around pears. Garnish with fresh mint sprigs and serve.

6 SERVINGS

if you can't stand the heat...

Do your oven-baked recipes often burn or come out undercooked? Chances are your oven needs calibrating—that is, its actual temperature measured so that you willl always know precisely what heat you are cooking at.

Use an oven thermometer to see if the control dial indicates the temperature accurately. Hanging spring-style thermometers have a reputation for breaking easily, so try a folding mercury oven thermometer—it stands in the bottom and is relatively inexpensive and more reliable. Look for them at cookware stores nationwide and in mail-order catalogs that carry assorted kitchen gadgets.

As it happens, many oven dials are slightly off, so make a habit of checking at least annually. To fine-tune the calibration, consult the manufacturer's instructions. For larger problems, a service call may be necessary. Some gas companies will calibrate gas ovens for their customers; check with your local company to find out whether this service is provided.

Flourless Chocolate Cake with Chocolate Glaze

CAKE
12 ounces bittersweet (not unsweetened) or semisweet chocolate, chopped
¾ cup (1½ sticks) unsalted butter, cut into pieces

6 large eggs, separated
12 tablespoons sugar
2 teaspoons vanilla extract

GLAZE
½ cup whipping cream
½ cup dark corn syrup
9 ounces bittersweet (not unsweetened) or semisweet chocolate, finely chopped

Chocolate shavings

FOR CAKE: Preheat oven to 350°F. Butter 9-inch-diameter springform pan. Line bottom of pan with parchment paper or waxed paper; butter paper. Wrap outside of pan with foil. Stir chocolate and butter in heavy medium saucepan over low heat until melted and smooth. Cool to lukewarm, stirring often.

Using electric mixer, beat egg yolks and 6 tablespoons sugar in large bowl until mixture is very thick and pale, about 3 minutes. Fold lukewarm chocolate mixture into yolk mixture, then fold in vanilla extract. Using clean dry beaters, beat egg whites in another large bowl until soft peaks form. Gradually add remaining 6 tablespoons sugar, beating until medium-firm peaks form. Fold whites into chocolate mixture in 3 additions. Pour batter into prepared pan.

Bake cake until top is puffed and cracked and tester inserted into center comes out with some moist crumbs attached, about

An intense chocolate cake with a soft center, this dessert is common on restaurant menus everywhere. It can be topped with ice cream and a chocolate or caramel sauce, paired with sorbet or a fruit compote, or finished with an elegant chocolate glaze, as it is here. No matter how you serve it, the cake is a simple, indulgent treat that's perfect for any occasion, any time of year.

50 minutes. Cool cake in pan on rack (cake will fall).

Gently press down crusty top to make evenly thick cake. Using small knife, cut around pan sides to loosen cake. Remove pan sides. Place 9-inch-diameter tart pan bottom or cardboard round atop cake. Invert cake onto tart pan bottom. Peel off parchment paper.

FOR GLAZE: Bring cream and corn syrup to simmer in medium saucepan. Remove from heat. Add chocolate; whisk until smooth.

Place cake on rack set over baking sheet. Spread ½ cup glaze smoothly over top and sides of cake. Freeze until almost set, about 3 minutes. Pour remaining glaze over cake; smooth sides and top. Place cake on platter. Chill until glaze is firm, 1 hour. *(Can be made 1 day ahead. Cover with cake dome; store at room temperature.)* Garnish with chocolate shavings. Serve at room temperature.

10 TO 12 SERVINGS

This impressive-looking, special-occasion cake has great orange and almond flavors—and lots of room for candles. Make it a day ahead of the party, if you like.

Orange-Almond Cake with Chocolate Icing

- 3 large oranges
- 2 cups plus 2 tablespoons all purpose flour
- 1 cup whole almonds
- 2 teaspoons baking powder
- ½ teaspoon salt
- 2 cups plus generous 1 tablespoon sugar

- 1 cup (2 sticks) unsalted butter, room temperature
- 4 large eggs
- 1 cup whole milk
- ½ teaspoon vanilla extract
- ¼ teaspoon almond extract

- 1½ cups fresh orange juice

Chocolate Icing (see recipe opposite)

Additional whole almonds
Small orange-slice triangles
Fresh mint leaves

Preheat oven to 350°F. Butter three 9-inch-diameter cake pans with 1½-inch-high sides. Dust with flour; tap out excess. Using vegetable peeler, remove peel (orange part only) in strips from oranges. Coarsely chop enough peel to measure ½ cup. Combine flour, 1 cup almonds, baking powder and salt in processor; blend until finely ground. Transfer to medium bowl. Place 2 cups sugar and orange peel in processor; blend until peel is finely minced.

Using electric mixer, beat butter in large bowl until smooth. Add sugar mixture and beat until fluffy. Beat in eggs 1 at a time. Mix milk and both extracts in small bowl. On low speed, beat flour mixture into egg mixture alternately with milk mixture in 3 additions each. Divide batter among prepared pans.

Bake cakes until tester inserted into center comes out clean, about 25 minutes. Cool cakes in pans on racks 5 minutes. Turn cakes out onto racks and cool completely.

Boil 1½ cups juice and remaining generous 1 tablespoon sugar in small saucepan until reduced to ½ cup, about 8 minutes. Brush warm juice mixture over tops of cooled cakes.

Place 1 cake layer, orange syrup side up, on cake platter. Spread 1 cup Chocolate Icing over. Top with second cake layer, then 1 cup icing. Top with third cake layer, syrup side up. Spread remaining icing over top and sides of cake. *(Can be prepared 1 day ahead. Cover with cake dome and store at room temperature.)*

Arrange additional almonds, orange triangles and mint leaves around top edge of cake. Slice cake and serve.

10 SERVINGS

Chocolate Icing

- 1¾ cups whipping cream
- ¾ cup (1½ sticks) unsalted butter
- 6 tablespoons unsweetened cocoa powder
- 4½ tablespoons light corn syrup
- 16 ounces bittersweet (not unsweetened) or semisweet chocolate, chopped
- 1½ teaspoons vanilla extract
- ½ teaspoon (scant) almond extract

Whisk first 4 ingredients in medium saucepan over medium heat until butter melts and mixture comes to simmer. Remove saucepan from heat. Add chocolate and both extracts. Whisk until chocolate is melted and smooth. Refrigerate frosting until slightly thickened but still spreadable, stirring occasionally, 45 minutes.

MAKES ABOUT 4 CUPS

birthday fiesta for eight

Margaritas

Grilled Chicken Drummettes with Ancho-Cherry Barbecue Sauce (page 22)

Tacos

Tossed Green Salad

Orange-Almond Cake with Chocolate Icing (opposite; pictured opposite)

Lemon Curd Layer Cake

Tall and beautiful, sweet and tart, this cake gets lots of flavor from a tangy lemon curd made from scratch. Begin this recipe at least a day ahead, or up to a week ahead if that's more convenient.

LEMON CURD

- 2⅓ cups sugar
- 2 teaspoons cornstarch
- 1 cup fresh lemon juice
- 4 large eggs
- 4 large egg yolks
- ¾ cup (1½ sticks) unsalted butter, cut into ½-inch pieces

FROSTING

- ¾ cup powdered sugar
- 2 cups chilled whipping cream

CAKE

- 1½ cups cake flour
- 1½ cups sugar
- 2½ teaspoons baking powder
- ¾ teaspoon salt
- 4 large egg yolks
- ¼ cup vegetable oil
- ¼ cup orange juice
- 1½ teaspoons grated lemon peel
- 8 large egg whites
- ¼ teaspoon cream of tartar

Lemon slices, halved, patted dry

FOR LEMON CURD: Combine 2⅓ cups sugar and 2 teaspoons cornstarch in heavy medium saucepan. Gradually whisk in fresh lemon juice. Whisk in eggs and yolks; add butter. Whisk over medium heat until curd thickens and boils, about 12 minutes. Pour into medium bowl. Refrigerate until cold, at least 5 hours. *(Can be prepared 1 week ahead. Cover and keep refrigerated.)*

FOR FROSTING: Beat powdered sugar and 1¼ cups lemon curd in large bowl just until blended. Beat cream in medium bowl until firm peaks form. Fold cream into curd mixture in 3 additions. Chill until firm, at least 4 hours.

FOR CAKE: Preheat oven to 350°F. Butter and flour three 9-inch-diameter cake pans with 1½-inch-high sides; line bottoms with parchment paper. Whisk 1½ cups cake flour, ½ cup sugar, 2½ teaspoons baking powder and ¾ teaspoon salt in large bowl. Add 4 yolks, ¼ cup vegetable oil, orange juice, lemon peel and ¾ cup curd to bowl (do not stir). Combine whites and ¼ teaspoon cream of tartar in another large bowl. Using electric mixer, beat whites until soft peaks form. Gradually add remaining 1 cup sugar, beating until stiff but not dry. Using same beaters, beat yolk mixture until smooth. Fold whites into yolk mixture in 3 additions.

Divide batter equally among prepared pans. Bake cakes until tester inserted into center comes out clean, about 25 minutes. Cool cakes in pans on racks 15 minutes. Turn cakes out onto racks; peel off parchment. Cool cakes completely.

Spoon 1 cup frosting into pastry bag fitted with plain round tip; refrigerate bag. Place 1 cake layer on cake platter. Spread top of cake layer with ⅓ cup curd, then 1 cup frosting. Top with second cake layer; spread with ⅓ cup curd and 1 cup frosting. Top with third cake layer. Spread remaining frosting over top and sides of cake. Spread remaining curd over top of cake, leaving ¾-inch plain border around edge. Pipe chilled 1 cup frosting in bag in small mounds around edge of cake. *(Cake can be prepared 1 day ahead; refrigerate.)* Place lemon slices between mounds of frosting.

8 TO 10 SERVINGS

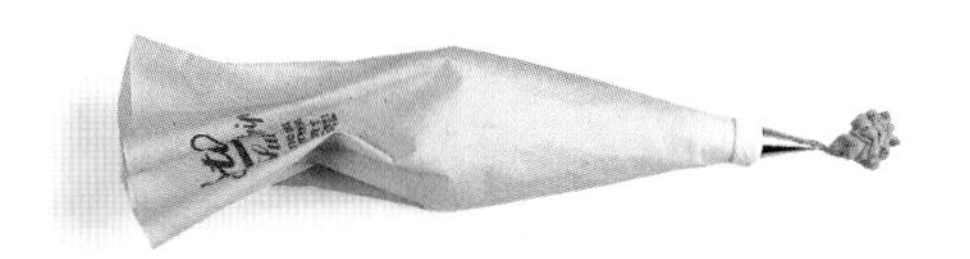

in the bag

When it comes to cake decorating, a pastry bag is indispensable. The bags come in lengths from 7 to 24 inches, and the most readily available are made from plastic-lined, canvas-like fabric and are sturdy and good for piping out firm mixtures. Next sturdiest is a plasticized nylon bag, sold at professional kitchenware shops. For flexibility and pliability, suppleness and ease of handling, nothing beats the nylon pastry bag, available at many kitchenware shops and through catalogs.

Tips, which are made from lightweight metal or plastic, come in a variety of styles and sizes. They slip easily into most bags and hold in place firmly. To use a small tip on a big bag, you will need to secure it with a coupler, a ring-shaped device that holds the tip in place.

Clean all pastry bags and tips thoroughly with lots of sudsy water after each use. Scrub the bag on the outside, then turn it inside out and scrub the inside too. Rinse well, then air-dry. The tips clean up easily with either a baby-bottle brush or a kid's-size toothbrush.

Triple-Cherry Cheesecake

Begin preparing this a day before you plan to serve it since the cheesecake needs to firm up overnight in the refrigerator. The do-ahead topping is made with dried cherries, Bing cherries and cherry jam for a triple dose of sweet fruit flavor.

TOPPING

- ¾ cup dried tart cherries
- 1 1-pound bag frozen pitted Bing cherries, thawed, drained, juice reserved
- ½ cup cherry jam
- 2 tablespoons brandy
- 1 tablespoon cornstarch

CRUST

- ⅓ cup whole almonds
- ⅔ cup graham cracker crumbs
- ¼ cup sugar
- ¼ cup (½ stick) unsalted butter, melted

FILLING

- 3 8-ounce packages cream cheese, room temperature
- 1⅓ cups sugar
- 4 large eggs
- 2 tablespoons fresh lemon juice
- ¼ teaspoon almond extract
- ¼ teaspoon salt
- ½ cup sliced almonds, toasted

FOR TOPPING: Combine dried cherries and reserved juice from thawed cherries in medium saucepan. Bring to boil. Remove from heat. Cover; let steep 20 minutes.

Mix jam, brandy and cornstarch in small bowl. Stir into dried cherry mixture. Add thawed cherries. Stir over medium heat until mixture thickens, about 1 minute. Cool slightly; chill until cold.

FOR CRUST: Finely grind almonds in processor. Add cracker crumbs, sugar and butter. Process until clumps form. Press mixture onto bottom (not sides) of 9-inch-diameter springform pan with 2¾-inch-high sides. Chill 30 minutes.

FOR FILLING: Position rack in center of oven; preheat to 350°F. Blend all ingredients except sliced almonds in processor just until smooth, scraping down sides of bowl several times. Transfer filling to crust. Bake until edges of cheesecake are puffed and center is just set, about 50 minutes. Remove from oven. Run knife around pan sides to loosen cake. Chill cake uncovered overnight.

Release pan sides from cake. Spoon topping over cake, leaving ½-inch border around edge. Garnish cake border with almonds.

10 SERVINGS

Butter Pecan Shortcakes with Caramelized Pineapple and Bananas

SHORTCAKES

- 2 cups unbleached all purpose flour
- 3 tablespoons sugar
- 2½ teaspoons baking powder
- ½ teaspoon salt
- ¼ teaspoon ground nutmeg
- 6 tablespoons (¾ stick) chilled unsalted butter, cut into small pieces
- ½ cup finely chopped pecans
- ½ cup whole milk
- 1 large egg
- ¼ cup chilled sour cream
- ½ teaspoon vanilla extract
- 1 egg yolk beaten with 1 tablespoon milk (for glaze)
- Additional sugar

FILLING

- 6 tablespoons (packed) golden brown sugar
- 3 tablespoons unsalted butter
- 1 20-ounce can pineapple slices in juice, drained well, patted dry, cut into ¾-inch pieces
- 2 large bananas, peeled, cut into ¼-inch-thick rounds
- Butter pecan ice cream

FOR SHORTCAKES: Position rack in center of oven and preheat to 425°F. Line large baking sheet with parchment. Sift first 5 ingredients into large bowl. Rub in butter with fingertips until mixture resembles very coarse meal. Mix in pecans. Whisk milk, 1 egg, sour cream and vanilla in small bowl to blend. Add to flour mixture and toss just until evenly moistened. Using about ½ cup dough per shortcake, drop dough onto prepared sheet in 6 mounds. Using floured hands, shape each mound into ball and return to sheet. Brush each with some egg glaze, then sprinkle with additional sugar. Bake until tester comes out clean, about 18 minutes. Transfer to rack; cool.

FOR FILLING: Whisk sugar and butter in heavy large skillet over medium-high heat until butter melts and mixture forms dark caramel sauce, 4 minutes. Add pineapple and bananas; stir gently until fruit is heated through, 2 minutes. Remove from heat. Cut shortcakes horizontally in half; place bottoms on 6 plates. Top with ice cream, then fruit. Lean tops against ice cream.

6 SERVINGS

Don't save shortcakes just for strawberry season. They're also delicious with other fruits, like the pineapple and banana combination here. To get a head start on this recipe, make the shortcakes four hours ahead, then rewarm them just before serving.

Lemon Mousse with Fresh Berries

Fresh strawberries, blueberries, raspberries and blackberries are used to their best advantage in this very pretty, fresh-tasting dessert. You can prepare all but the whipped cream topping a day ahead.

1 cup plus 1 tablespoon sugar
¾ cup fresh lemon juice
6 large egg yolks
2 large eggs
1½ tablespoons grated lemon peel

1 12-ounce basket strawberries, hulled, halved (or quartered if large)
1 6-ounce basket fresh blueberries
1 6-ounce basket fresh raspberries
1 6-ounce basket fresh blackberries

2 cups chilled whipping cream

8 whole strawberries (for garnish)
Fresh mint sprigs

Combine 1 cup sugar, lemon juice, yolks, eggs and lemon peel in large metal bowl. Set bowl over saucepan of simmering water (do not allow bowl to touch water). Whisk until mixture thickens and thermometer inserted into mixture registers 160°F. Transfer lemon curd to another large bowl. Chill until cool, whisking occasionally.

Toss halved strawberries, blueberries, raspberries, blackberries and remaining 1 tablespoon sugar in another large bowl.

Using electric mixer, beat 1½ cups cream in medium bowl until medium-firm peaks form. Fold ⅓ of whipped cream into lemon curd to lighten, then fold in remaining whipped cream.

Divide berry mixture among 8 dessert bowls or wineglasses. Spoon lemon mousse over. *(Can be made 1 day ahead. Cover; chill.)*

Using electric mixer, beat remaining ½ cup cream in medium bowl until stiff peaks form. Spoon whipped cream atop desserts or transfer whipped cream to pastry bag fitted with large star tip and pipe atop desserts. Garnish with whole strawberries and mint.

8 SERVINGS

Coconut Flan

- 1 14-ounce can sweetened condensed milk
- 1⅓ cups whole milk
- 2 large eggs
- 2 large egg yolks
- ½ teaspoon vanilla extract
- ¾ cup sweetened flaked coconut

Preheat oven to 350°F. Arrange six ¾-cup custard cups in 13 x 9 x 2-inch baking pan. Whisk first 5 ingredients in medium bowl to blend. Mix in coconut. Divide mixture among cups. Pour enough hot water into pan to come halfway up sides of cups.

Bake flans until just set in center, about 30 minutes. Remove flans from pan and refrigerate until cold, about 2 hours. *(Can be prepared 1 day ahead. Cover and keep refrigerated.)*

6 SERVINGS

This flan, which is sweetened with flaked coconut, comes together in a flash. It bakes for just 30 minutes and then chills until cold, about two hours. An added bonus: It can be made up to a day ahead.

Irish Cream Pudding Parfaits with Oatmeal-Walnut Crunch

The oatmeal and nut mixture in this dessert is reminiscent of the topping on a fruit crisp; here, it is cooked until crisp, then layered with currants and a custard made with Baileys Original Irish Cream.

CRUNCH

1 cup old-fashioned oats
¾ cup all purpose flour
½ cup (packed) golden brown sugar
2 teaspoons instant coffee crystals
¼ teaspoon ground allspice
¼ teaspoon salt
½ cup (1 stick) chilled unsalted butter, cut into ½-inch pieces
¾ cup coarsely chopped walnuts

PUDDING

1¼ cups chilled whipping cream
12 tablespoons Baileys Original Irish Cream or other Irish cream liqueur
¾ cup (packed) golden brown sugar
6 large egg yolks
¼ teaspoon ground nutmeg

12 tablespoons dried currants

FOR CRUNCH: Preheat oven to 350°F. Combine first 6 ingredients in large bowl. Add butter and rub in with fingertips until mixture forms moist clumps. Mix in walnuts. Sprinkle mixture onto rimmed baking sheet. Bake until golden brown and crisp, occasionally stirring gently and leaving mixture in clumps, about 35 minutes. Cool completely. *(Can be made 2 days ahead. Store airtight.)*

FOR PUDDING: Combine ¾ cup cream, 6 tablespoons Baileys liqueur, sugar, yolks and nutmeg in large metal bowl. Place over saucepan of simmering water (do not allow bottom of bowl to touch water). Using electric mixer, beat until custard thickens and thermometer registers 160°F, about 8 minutes. Remove from over water and beat until cool, about 8 minutes. Mix in remaining 6 tablespoons liqueur. Beat remaining ½ cup cream in medium bowl to medium peaks. Fold into custard. Cover; chill 4 hours or overnight.

Layer ¼ cup pudding, 1 tablespoon currants and 3 tablespoons crunch in each of six 12-ounce goblets; repeat layering 1 more time. Serve immediately or refrigerate up to 1 hour.

6 SERVINGS

Mocha Custards

¾ cup sugar
8 large egg yolks
1 tablespoon coffee liqueur
½ teaspoon vanilla extract
3 cups half and half
½ ounce semisweet chocolate, finely grated
1½ tablespoons instant coffee powder

Whipped cream
Chocolate coffee bean candies

Preheat oven to 325°F. Arrange six ¾-cup soufflé dishes or custard cups in 13 x 9 x 2-inch baking pan. Using wooden spoon, stir sugar, yolks, liqueur and vanilla extract in medium bowl to blend well. Stir half and half, chocolate and coffee powder in heavy medium saucepan over medium heat until chocolate melts and mixture just comes to simmer. Very gradually stir hot mocha mixture into yolk mixture. Strain custard into spouted measuring cup; pour custard into soufflé dishes.

Pour enough hot water into pan to come halfway up sides of dishes. Bake custards until just set in center when pan is gently shaken, about 45 minutes. Transfer custards to rack; cool 1 hour. Cover and refrigerate until very cold, about 4 hours. *(Can be prepared 1 day ahead. Keep refrigerated.)*

Top custards with whipped cream and coffee bean candies.

6 SERVINGS

There's just a hint of chocolate in these creamy mocha custards. For a garnish, top with chocolate-covered coffee bean candies, which you can find in candy shops, specialty foods stores and supermarkets.

Ginger and Vanilla Bean Crème Brûlée

Before baking the custards, pour hot water into the pan until it comes halfway up the sides of the dishes. Using this method, called a *bain-marie* or water bath, keeps the custards from curdling by cooking them gently until they are set.

Hold the blowtorch two inches from the layer of sugar on top of the chilled custards. The heat melts and burns the sugar, which forms a crisp layer as it cools.

CUSTARD

2 cups whipping cream
½ cup sugar
2 tablespoons chopped peeled fresh ginger
1 vanilla bean, split lengthwise

5 large egg yolks

TOPPING

12 teaspoons sugar
Sliced tropical fruit (such as mango, papaya and/or kiwi)

FOR CUSTARD: Preheat oven to 325°F. Place three 4-inch-diameter fluted flan dishes* in each of two 13 x 9 x 2-inch baking pans or place six ¾-cup ramekins in 1 pan.

Mix cream, sugar and ginger in heavy medium saucepan. Using small sharp knife, scrape seeds from vanilla bean. Add seeds and bean to saucepan. Stir over medium heat until sugar dissolves and mixture comes to simmer. Cover pan, reduce heat to very low and simmer gently 10 minutes. Strain into large measuring cup.

Whisk yolks in medium bowl until well blended. Gradually whisk in hot cream mixture just to blend. Return custard to measuring cup; divide among dishes. Pour enough hot water into pans to come halfway up sides of dishes. Carefully transfer pans to oven.

Bake custards until almost set in center when pans are gently shaken, about 30 minutes for fluted flan dishes and 35 minutes for ramekins. Using metal spatula, transfer custards in dishes to work surface; cool 30 minutes. Chill at least 3 hours and up to 2 days.

FOR TOPPING: Sprinkle 2 teaspoons sugar evenly over each custard. Broil custards in preheated broiler until sugar melts and browns or, working with 1 custard at a time, hold blowtorch** so that flame is 2 inches above surface. Direct flame so that sugar melts and browns, about 2 minutes. Refrigerate until custards are firm again but topping is still brittle, at least 2 hours but no longer than 4 hours so that topping doesn't soften. Garnish with fruit.

**Four-inch-diameter fluted clear glass flan dishes are available at cookware stores and many hardware stores. They are about ⅔ inch deep and hold about ½ cup liquid.*

***Available at some cookware stores.*

6 SERVINGS

Cherry-Almond Trifle

This take on a traditional English trifle has a rich vanilla custard layered between fresh cherry jam and almond-flavored cake. The custard needs to chill for a day, so begin preparing this recipe at least a day ahead.

JAM

2 cups fresh cherries (about 12 ounces), pitted, coarsely chopped
1 cup sugar
¼ cup water

CAKE

1 7-ounce package almond paste, cut into small pieces
1¼ cups sugar
1¼ cups (2½ sticks) unsalted butter, cut into pieces
2 teaspoons vanilla extract
6 large eggs
1 cup all purpose flour
1½ teaspoons baking powder
¼ teaspoon salt

CUSTARD

½ cup sugar
2 tablespoons cornstarch
6 large egg yolks
2 teaspoons vanilla extract
2 cups half and half

3 cups fresh cherries (about 18 ounces), pitted, coarsely chopped

1 cup chilled whipping cream
¼ cup powdered sugar
Cherries with stems
Slivered almonds, toasted

FOR JAM: Combine all ingredients in heavy medium saucepan. Stir over medium heat until sugar dissolves and mixture boils. Reduce heat to medium-low and simmer until jam is thick, stirring often, 22 minutes. Transfer to small bowl. Cover; chill up to 3 days.

FOR CAKE: Preheat oven to 325°F. Butter 9-inch-diameter springform pan. Line bottom with parchment; butter parchment. Blend almond paste and sugar in processor until mixture resembles fine meal, about 1 minute. Add butter and vanilla and blend well, occasionally scraping down sides of bowl. Blend in eggs 1 at a time. Using on/off turns, blend in flour, baking powder and salt (do not overmix). Transfer batter to prepared pan.

Place pan on baking sheet; bake cake until tester inserted into center comes out clean and top is golden, 1 hour 10 minutes. Cool cake in pan on rack. Cover; keep at room temperature 1 day.

FOR CUSTARD: Whisk ½ cup sugar and cornstarch in heavy medium saucepan to blend. Beat in yolks and vanilla. Gradually whisk in half and half. Stir over medium heat until custard thickens and boils. Transfer to bowl. Press plastic wrap directly onto surface of custard; refrigerate custard 1 day.

Cut around pan sides to loosen cake; release pan sides. Cut cake horizontally into 3 layers; discard parchment. Spoon thin layer of custard over bottom of 3- to 3½-quart trifle bowl. Trim 1 cake layer to fit, if necessary; place in bowl. Spread with ⅓ of custard. Mix chopped cherries into jam. Spoon ⅓ of jam mixture atop custard; spread to edge of bowl so that jam shows. Top with second cake layer, half of remaining custard and half of remaining jam mixture; spread to edge of bowl. Top with third cake layer. Spread with remaining custard, then remaining jam mixture.

Beat cream and powdered sugar until stiff peaks form. Transfer to pastry bag fitted with star tip. Pipe cream in center of trifle. Pipe rosettes around edge; top with whole cherries. Sprinkle trifle with almonds. Cover; chill at least 3 hours and up to 1 day.

10 TO 12 SERVINGS

measuring cups

To ensure a recipe's success, it's important to use the right measuring equipment. For dry ingredients, you need sturdy metal measuring cups that will keep their shape through thousands of dips into the sugar bin. They should also have straight sides, allowing you to level them off for precise measurements. A basic set comprises cups in four sizes: ¼ cup, ⅓ cup, ½ cup and 1 cup. Some sets include two other measures: a ⅛-cup measure and a 2-cup measure.

Liquid should not be measured in dry measuring cups. If the cup is filled to the rim, the center of the liquid can swell slightly without overflowing, resulting in an inaccuracy of up to a tablespoon per cup. Liquid measuring cups are calibrated in cups, ounces and milliliters, and include pouring spouts. They should be made of clear glass, so you can set the cup on the counter, bend down so it is at eye level, and pour in the liquid. Pyrex cups, the most common brand, are heat-resistant, making them ideal for bringing measured liquids to a boil or melting chocolate in a microwave oven.

Strawberry and Champagne Ice

Errata: This is the correct text for the sidenote on page 184:

An ice, which is distinguished from a sorbet by its granular texture, is one of the simplest and most refreshing desserts. Here, the classic combination of Champagne and strawberry provides flavor.

- ¾ cup plus 2 tablespoons sugar
- ¾ cup water

- 5¼ cups hulled fresh strawberries (about three 12-ounce baskets), halved

- 1 tablespoon light corn syrup
- 2 teaspoons fresh lemon juice
- 2 teaspoons vanilla extract

- 1½ cups cold extra-dry Champagne

- Fresh mint sprigs

Stir ¾ cup sugar and ¾ cup water in heavy small saucepan over medium heat until sugar dissolves. Bring to simmer. Remove from heat; cool sugar syrup completely.

Puree 3 cups strawberries in blender just until smooth. Strain puree through fine strainer.

Transfer sugar syrup and 1½ cups strawberry puree to large bowl (reserve any remaining puree for another use). Stir in corn syrup, lemon juice and vanilla. Refrigerate mixture until cold, 2 hours.

Stir Champagne into strawberry mixture. Process in ice cream maker according to manufacturer's instructions. Transfer strawberry ice to covered container; freeze until firm, at least 4 hours. *(Can be prepared 1 day ahead. Keep strawberry ice frozen. Cover and refrigerate remaining strawberries.)*

Toss remaining 2¼ cups strawberries with 2 tablespoons sugar in large bowl. Let stand until juices form, about 1 hour. Divide strawberries among 6 dessert cups. Top each serving with 1 scoop strawberry ice. Garnish with mint sprigs.

MAKES ABOUT 4 CUPS

Lemon Sorbet with Blackberry Sauce

1 pound frozen unsweetened blackberries, unthawed
5 tablespoons sugar

3 pints lemon sorbet

Place frozen berries in large bowl. Sprinkle sugar over berries; let stand until berries are just thawed but still cold, about 1 hour. Using fork, coarsely mash berries. *(Can be made 4 hours ahead. Cover blackberry sauce and refrigerate.)*

Spoon sorbet into dessert glasses. Top with blackberry sauce.

10 SERVINGS

Peach-Amaretto Sundaes

2 pints vanilla ice cream, softened slightly
5 tablespoons amaretto
2 tablespoons brandy

6 ripe peaches, peeled if desired, pitted, cut into ½-inch-thick slices
¼ cup sugar

1 cup crushed amaretti cookies (Italian macaroons)*

Combine ice cream, 3 tablespoons amaretto and 1 tablespoon brandy in large bowl. Stir to blend well. Cover and freeze until firm. *(Can be prepared 2 days ahead. Keep ice cream mixture frozen.)*

Combine peaches, sugar, remaining 2 tablespoons amaretto and 1 tablespoon brandy in another large bowl. Toss to coat. Let peach mixture stand until sugar dissolves, tossing occasionally, 15 minutes.

Divide sliced peaches among 6 dessert bowls or wineglasses. Spoon vanilla ice cream mixture atop peaches. Sprinkle desserts with crushed amaretti cookies. Serve immediately.

*Amaretti *are crisp Italian macaroons. They are available at Italian markets and in some supermarkets.*

6 SERVINGS

Juicy peaches, crushed *amaretti* cookies and vanilla ice cream spiked with brandy and amaretto add up to a perfect treat.

Chocolate-Cherry Ice Cream Loaf

- 2 pints cherry vanilla ice cream, softened slightly
- 1 cup almonds, toasted, chopped
- 3 tablespoons chopped drained maraschino cherries
- 1½ pints chocolate-chocolate chip ice cream, softened slightly

- 1¾ cups whipping cream
- ¼ cup light corn syrup
- 24 ounces bittersweet (not unsweetened) or semisweet chocolate, chopped
- 6 ounces semisweet chocolate, chopped
- 2 teaspoons vanilla extract
- ½ teaspoon almond extract

Line 9 x 5 x 2½-inch metal loaf pan with plastic wrap, leaving 3-inch overhang on all sides. Using small flexible spatula, quickly spread softened cherry vanilla ice cream evenly over bottom and up sides of prepared pan. Freeze until firm, about 30 minutes. Sprinkle ¼ cup chopped almonds, then maraschino cherries over ice cream in bottom of pan. Spread softened chocolate-chocolate chip ice cream over, filling pan completely. Freeze until firm, 1 hour.

Bring 1½ cups cream and corn syrup to simmer in medium saucepan. Remove from heat. Add both chocolates and whisk until smooth. Whisk in both extracts. Cool ganache to room temperature, whisking occasionally, about 45 minutes.

Spread ⅔ cup chocolate ganache over top of ice cream. Freeze until chocolate is very firm, about 2 hours.

Rewarm chocolate ganache over low heat just until fluid, if necessary. Cool to room temperature (mixture will thicken slightly). Line baking sheet with waxed paper. Run small knife around sides of loaf pan to loosen ice cream loaf. Invert loaf onto prepared sheet; peel off plastic wrap. Working quickly and using small flexible spatula, spread 1 cup chocolate ganache over top and sides of ice cream loaf, covering ice cream completely and forming ¼-inch-thick coating (reserve remaining ganache). Sprinkle ¾ cup chopped almonds over top and sides of chocolate-covered ice cream loaf. Freeze until chocolate is firm, 1 hour. *(Can be made 1 week ahead. Cover with plastic wrap; keep frozen. Chill remaining ganache.)*

Add remaining ¼ cup cream to ganache and rewarm over low heat to use as sauce. Cut loaf into ½-inch-thick slices. Cut each slice diagonally in half, forming 2 triangles. Place 2 triangles on each plate. Drizzle with warm ganache and serve.

8 TO 10 SERVINGS

frozen domes

Any ice cream, gelato, sherbet, sorbet, or ice—alone or combined with others—can be shaped inside a mold and then, just before serving, unmolded for a spectacular presentation. Several such frozen desserts have been given special descriptive names to reflect their appearance:

- Baked Alaska: For this fanciful hot-and-cold dessert, a molded block of frozen ice cream is covered in meringue and then quickly baked to brown the meringue before serving.
- Bombe: Formed in a bomblike metal canister, this dessert usually features concentric layers of two or more flavors. (The loaf is a variation.)
- Frozen soufflé: Formed in and served from a soufflé dish, complete with a paper collar to let it rise above the rim, this frozen dessert combines different-colored layers of parfait (a frozen custard made with beaten egg yolks, sugar and whipped cream).
- Tartufo: This individually sized frozen dessert coats a ball of ice cream with cocoa powder or grated chocolate to make it resemble a truffle, from which it takes its Italian name.

Black-and-White Ice Cream Sandwiches

Mint chip ice cream (or the flavor of your choice) is the tasty filling between tender chocolate cookies that have been dipped halfway into white chocolate.

- 2 pints mint chocolate chip ice cream, softened slightly
- ¾ cup (1½ sticks) unsalted butter, room temperature
- ½ cup plus 2 tablespoons sugar
- 1 large egg yolk
- 1 teaspoon vanilla extract
- 1¼ cups all purpose flour
- ¼ cup unsweetened cocoa powder (preferably Dutch-process)
- ¼ teaspoon salt
- 10 ounces good-quality white chocolate (such as Lindt or Baker's), chopped

Drop six ⅔-cup mounds mint chocolate chip ice cream onto waxed-paper-lined baking sheet. Using metal spatula, shape each mound into 3- to 3½-inch square; freeze squares. Beat butter and sugar in large bowl until smooth. Beat in egg yolk and vanilla. Sift flour, cocoa and salt onto butter mixture. Stir until blended and soft dough forms. Gather dough into ball; flatten into rectangle. Roll out dough between 2 sheets of waxed paper to 13 x 10-inch rectangle. Place dough, still between waxed paper sheets, on baking sheet. Chill at least 1 hour and up to 1 day.

Position rack in center of oven and preheat to 300°F. Line large baking sheet with parchment paper. Peel top sheet of waxed paper off dough. Trim dough to 12 x 9-inch rectangle; cut dough into twelve 3-inch squares. Transfer squares to parchment-lined sheet, discarding waxed paper and spacing squares about 1 inch apart. Bake until cookies are firm to touch, 20 minutes. Cool cookies on sheet.

Melt white chocolate in medium metal bowl set over saucepan of barely simmering water, stirring until smooth (do not allow bottom of bowl to touch water). Remove bowl from over water.

Holding corner of 1 cookie, dip cookie into melted chocolate until half covered on diagonal, tilting bowl if necessary to submerge. Shake cookie gently to allow some excess chocolate to drip back into bowl. Return dipped cookie to parchment-lined baking sheet. Repeat with remaining cookies and white chocolate. Freeze cookies until chocolate coating is firm, about 10 minutes.

Arrange 6 cookies, flat side up, on work surface. Top each with frozen ice cream square, then another cookie, flat side down, pressing slightly to adhere. Cover and freeze up to 4 days.

MAKES 6

S'mores Sundaes

- 1 cup whole wheat flour
- 1 cup (packed) golden brown sugar
- 1 teaspoon baking powder
- ¼ teaspoon salt
- ½ cup (1 stick) unsalted butter, melted
- 1 large egg
- 1 teaspoon vanilla extract
- ¾ cup chopped walnuts

- ¾ cup whipping cream
- 5 ounces bittersweet (not unsweetened) or semisweet chocolate, chopped

- 16 large marshmallows
- 1½ pints coffee ice cream

Here is a delicious interpretation of a campfire classic. There are still the requisite marshmallows and chocolate (in the form of a homemade chocolate sauce), but instead of graham crackers, this recipe uses chewy baked blondies as a base, topped with scoops of coffee ice cream.

Preheat oven to 350°F. Lightly butter 8-inch square baking pan. Mix flour, brown sugar, baking powder and salt in medium bowl. Whisk butter, egg and vanilla in large bowl to blend. Add flour mixture. Stir to blend. Mix in nuts. Press dough over bottom of prepared pan. Bake blondie until golden and tester inserted into center comes out clean, about 25 minutes. Transfer pan to rack and cool.

Bring cream to simmer in heavy small saucepan. Remove from heat. Add chocolate. Stir until chocolate melts and mixture is smooth. *(Can be made 1 day ahead. Store blondie airtight at room temperature. Cover and refrigerate chocolate sauce. Rewarm sauce over medium-low heat before using.)*

Cut blondie into 16 squares. Place 2 squares in each of 8 large sundae dishes. Thread marshmallows onto 4 skewers; hold over gas flame or under broiler until soft and golden. Place 2 scoops ice cream atop blondies. Spoon sauce over. Top with marshmallows.

8 SERVINGS

Double-Decker Rhubarb Ice Cream Sandwiches

Make these with fresh rhubarb when it is in season (late winter through midsummer), then with the frozen variety at other times of the year. The pistachio meringues can be prepared up to a week ahead and frozen.

1 vanilla bean, split lengthwise
5 cups ½-inch-thick slices trimmed fresh rhubarb or one 1¼-pound bag frozen unsweetened rhubarb, thawed, with juices
1½ cups sugar
4 tablespoons light corn syrup
Pinch of salt
1 cup frozen unsweetened raspberries, thawed, with juices

6 large egg yolks
½ cup whipping cream

24 Pistachio Meringues (see recipe opposite)

Scrape seeds from vanilla bean into heavy medium saucepan; add bean. Add rhubarb (with juices if using frozen), 1 cup sugar, 2 tablespoons corn syrup and pinch of salt. Cover pan and cook over medium-low heat until rhubarb is tender, about 10 minutes. Cool; discard vanilla bean. Place rhubarb mixture in blender. Add raspberries with juices; puree mixture until smooth.

Whisk egg yolks, ½ cup whipping cream, remaining ½ cup sugar and 2 tablespoons corn syrup in clean heavy medium saucepan to

blend well. Stir mixture over medium-low heat until thick enough to coat spoon, about 7 minutes (do not boil). Remove from heat. Mix in 2⅔ cups rhubarb-raspberry puree. Refrigerate custard until cold. Cover and chill remaining rhubarb-raspberry puree for sauce.

Process rhubarb custard in ice cream maker according to manufacturer's instructions. Freeze in covered container.

Place 8 Pistachio Meringues on clean baking sheet. Top each meringue with scoop of rhubarb-raspberry ice cream; flatten ice cream to reach edge of meringue. Top each ice-cream-covered meringue with another meringue and another scoop of ice cream; flatten to reach edge. Top each with third meringue. Cover and freeze ice cream sandwiches until firm, at least 2 hours. *(Can be prepared 3 days ahead. Keep frozen.)*

Cut sandwiches in half. Place 2 halves, rounded sides down, on plates. Drizzle with reserved puree and serve.

8 SERVINGS

Pistachio Meringues

- 1¼ cups shelled natural pistachios, chopped
- ½ cup powdered sugar
- 3 large egg whites
- ¼ teaspoon cream of tartar
- ⅔ cup sugar

Preheat oven to 225°F. Line 2 large baking sheets with aluminum foil; butter and flour foil. Mix pistachios and powdered sugar in small bowl to blend. Beat egg whites and cream of tartar in medium bowl until soft peaks form. Gradually add sugar, beating until whites are stiff but not dry. Fold nut mixture into egg whites. Drop meringue onto prepared sheets by rounded tablespoonfuls, spacing 1 inch apart and spreading to form 2½-inch rounds.

Bake meringues until dry and almost crisp but not yet colored, about 45 minutes. Cool meringues on baking sheets. *(Can be prepared 1 week ahead. Wrap airtight in foil and freeze.)*

MAKES ABOUT 24

lunch on the lawn for four

Black Currant Iced Tea with Cinnamon and Ginger (page 35)

Baked Artichokes with Crab and Sourdough Stuffing (page 206)

Mixed Baby Greens with Lemon Vinaigrette

Crusty Rolls

Double-Decker Rhubarb Ice Cream Sandwiches (opposite; pictured opposite)

Dark Chocolate Brownies with White Chocolate Chunks

Nobody can resist brownies, especially when they're studded with chunks of white chocolate and served with fresh strawberries. (Make these a day ahead, if you like.)

4 ounces unsweetened chocolate, coarsely chopped
6 tablespoons (¾ stick) unsalted butter

⅔ cup all purpose flour
½ teaspoon baking powder
¼ teaspoon salt
1 cup sugar
2 large eggs
1 teaspoon vanilla extract
5 ounces good-quality white chocolate (such as Lindt or Baker's), cut into ½-inch pieces

Fresh large strawberries

Preheat oven to 325°F. Butter 8-inch square baking pan. Stir chocolate and butter in heavy medium saucepan over low heat until melted and smooth. Cool to room temperature.

Combine ⅔ cup flour, ½ teaspoon baking powder and ¼ teaspoon salt in small bowl. Whisk 1 cup sugar, eggs and vanilla extract in medium bowl until mixture is very thick, about 3 minutes. Whisk in melted chocolate mixture, then flour mixture. Stir in white chocolate. Transfer to prepared pan.

Bake brownies until tester inserted into center comes out with moist crumbs attached, about 28 minutes. Transfer brownies in pan to rack; cool completely. *(Can be prepared 1 day ahead. Store airtight at room temperature.)*

Cut brownies into 16 squares. Serve with strawberries.

MAKES 16

Ginger-Molasses Cookies

- 2½ cups all purpose flour
- 1 tablespoon baking soda
- 1 teaspoon ground ginger
- ½ teaspoon salt
- 1 cup (packed) dark brown sugar
- ½ cup solid vegetable shortening, room temperature
- ½ cup mild-flavored (light) molasses
- 2 teaspoons instant espresso powder dissolved in 1 tablespoon hot water
- 1 large egg
- 1½ teaspoons vanilla extract
- Sugar

Whisk first 4 ingredients in medium bowl. Using electric mixer, beat brown sugar, shortening and molasses in large bowl until well blended. Beat in espresso mixture, egg and vanilla. Mix in dry ingredients. Cover and refrigerate dough until firm, about 4 hours. *(Can be prepared 1 day ahead. Keep refrigerated.)*

Preheat oven to 350°F. Butter 2 large baking sheets. Using wet hands, form dough into 1¼-inch balls, then roll in sugar to coat evenly. Working in batches, arrange balls on prepared baking sheets, spacing 2 inches apart. Bake cookies until cracked on top but center is softly set, about 12 minutes. Transfer cookies to rack and cool. *(Can be made 1 day ahead. Store in airtight container.)*

MAKES ABOUT 3½ DOZEN

the sweet truth about sugar

Sugar doesn't deserve all of its evil reputation. Contrary to popular belief, it is not entirely to blame for obesity (dietary fat is usually a co-conspirator); and although it may trigger short bursts of energy, sugar doesn't cause hyperactivity. The only valid charge leveled against sugar is that it promotes tooth decay.

That is not to say that sugar is good for you. This sweet form of carbohydrate adds very little to the diet other than calories—as many as 48 per tablespoon. But figuring out a product's sugar content by reading the ingredients label isn't always easy. Generally speaking, any term ending in *–ose* (such as sucrose, fructose, maltose, dextrose and lactose) denotes a form of sugar. Other types include sweeteners touted as "natural," like maple syrup, fruit juices, brown sugar and honey.

For the real scoop, read product labels a little more carefully—and don't forget to brush and floss after eating those *oses*.

Cream Cheese Strudel Cookies

1 cup all purpose flour
4 ounces chilled cream cheese, cut into ½-inch pieces
½ cup (1 stick) chilled unsalted butter, cut into ½-inch pieces

½ cup apricot jam
1 cup sweetened flaked coconut
1 cup dried tart or Bing cherries

These tender cookies have cream cheese in the dough and an apricot, coconut and dried cherry filling. They're a delicious afternoon treat with a cup of tea.

Combine first 3 ingredients in processor; blend until clumps form. Gather dough into ball; flatten into square. Wrap in plastic; freeze until cold enough to roll, 15 minutes, or chill up to 1 day.

Preheat oven to 375°F. Butter baking sheet. Cut dough crosswise in half. Roll out each piece on floured surface to 12 x 8-inch rectangle. Spread each with ¼ cup jam. Top each with ½ cup coconut and ½ cup cherries. Starting at 1 long side, roll dough up jelly-roll style; seal long seam. Cut each roll crosswise into 12 pieces. Arrange pieces, cut side up, on prepared baking sheet. Flatten each cookie to ½-inch thickness.

Bake cookies until golden, about 25 minutes. Cool on rack.

MAKES ABOUT 2 DOZEN

Twice-baked Almond Cookies

2½ cups all purpose flour
Pinch of salt
1¼ cups sugar
3 large eggs
2 tablespoons honey
1 tablespoon orange flower water*
2¼ cups whole almonds (about 12 ounces)

Position rack in center of oven and preheat to 425°F. Butter and flour 13 x 9 x 2-inch metal baking pan. Sift flour and salt into medium bowl. Whisk sugar, eggs, honey and orange flower water in large bowl to blend well. Gradually add flour mixture, stirring just until blended. Stir in almonds. Spoon batter into prepared pan. Using back of spoon, spread batter evenly to smooth top.

The almonds in these twice-baked cookies provide extra crunch. Orange flower water adds an exotic note of citrus. Make them up to five days ahead, since they keep well.

Bake until dough puffs and is pale golden, about 20 minutes. Cool pastry in pan 5 minutes. Turn pastry out onto rack; cool completely. Maintain oven temperature.

Cut pastry crosswise into ½-inch-wide strips. Cut each strip diagonally into 3 pieces. Arrange cookies, cut side down, on 2 baking sheets. Bake until cookies are golden, about 14 minutes. Transfer cookies to racks; cool. *(Can be prepared 5 days ahead. Store airtight at room temperature.)*

**Orange flower water is an extract sold at liquor stores and in the liquor or specialty foods section of some supermarkets.*

MAKES ABOUT 6 DOZEN

❖

These walnut-topped treats, which can be prepared up to two days ahead, have an appealing sandy texture. They're especially good with a cup of coffee.

Walnut-topped Spice Cookies

- ½ cup vegetable oil
- ½ cup sugar
- 1 tablespoon creamy peanut butter
- ½ teaspoon ground cinnamon
- ¼ teaspoon ground cloves
- ¼ teaspoon almond extract
- ¼ teaspoon salt
- 1½ cups all purpose flour
- 18 (about) walnut halves
- 1 egg, beaten to blend (for glaze)

Preheat oven to 325°F. Line baking sheet with foil. Beat first 7 ingredients in large bowl to blend. Mix in flour. Shape dough into walnut-size balls; arrange 1 inch apart on prepared sheet. Top each with 1 walnut half. Press walnuts to adhere to dough and to flatten balls slightly. Brush generously with glaze.

Bake cookies until cooked through and light brown, about 20 minutes. Cool on sheet. *(Can be prepared 2 days ahead. Store cookies airtight at room temperature.)*

MAKES ABOUT 1½ DOZEN

Lemon Butter Cookies

- ¾ cup (1½ sticks) unsalted butter, room temperature
- ⅔ cup sugar
- 2 tablespoons finely grated lemon peel
- 1 large egg
- 1 teaspoon vanilla extract
- ¼ teaspoon (generous) salt
- 2 cups all purpose flour

Powdered sugar

Old-fashioned butter cookies get a twist with the addition of lemon peel. The recipe calls for using a heart-shaped cookie cutter, but feel free to use any shape you desire.

Using electric mixer, beat butter in large bowl until light. Beat in sugar and lemon peel. Add egg, 1 teaspoon vanilla extract and salt. Beat mixture until well blended. Add flour, 1 cup at a time, beating just until blended after each addition. Gather dough into ball; divide in half. Flatten each half into disk. Wrap in plastic and refrigerate until firm, about 30 minutes.

Preheat oven to 375°F. Roll out 1 dough disk on well-floured surface to ¼-inch thickness. Cut out cookies using 2½- to 2¾-inch heart-shaped cookie cutter. Gather scraps, reroll and cut out additional cookies. Transfer cookies to 2 ungreased baking sheets, spacing ½ inch apart. Bake cookies until golden brown around edges, about 8 minutes. Transfer cookies to rack; cool 30 minutes. Sift powdered sugar over cookies. Repeat with remaining dough disk. *(Can be made 1 day ahead. Store airtight at room temperature.)*

MAKES ABOUT 3 DOZEN

Clockwise from above: Spaghetti with Sicilian Meatballs (page 205); Southwest-Style Salisbury Steaks (page 201); Oysters Rockefeller (page 200); Hazelnut-crusted Goat Cheese Salad (page 214).

the american century in food

As the calendar marched ahead, we at *Bon Appétit* found ourselves looking back—as far back as the beginning of the century—to learn more about the evolution of cooking in this country. We wanted to know how what we ate when helped define the times. The result was a decade-by-decade look, "The American Century in Food," a special issue of the magazine. The best of that issue makes up this new section, a collection of truly memorable American dishes, all of them updated for today's tastes.

Flip through the pages that follow and you'll witness the century unfolding through a cavalcade of all-American recipes, from Oysters Rockefeller (page 200), an appetizer that dates back to the first part of the century, to Wild Mushroom Risotto (page 218), an international example of how this decade defines comfort food. Along the way, you'll discover that, as much as food has changed over the past hundred years, those dishes that sustained us through the bad times and helped us celebrate the good times remain inherently appealing.

A new century awaits, but this last one, as you'll see and remember here, was just plain delicious.

Oysters Rockefeller

The original recipe for oysters Rockefeller, created at the New Orleans restaurant Antoine's in 1899, remains a secret to this day. The appetizer, oysters topped with a mixture of finely chopped greens and copious amounts of butter and then baked in their shells, was considered so rich that it had to be named after the richest man of the day, John D. Rockefeller. A few years later, no self-respecting restaurateur would be without his own version on the menu. This lighter take features spinach, watercress, green onions and freshly grated Parmesan cheese.

- 1 garlic clove
- 2 cups loosely packed fresh spinach
- 1 bunch watercress, stems trimmed
- ½ cup chopped green onions

- ¾ cup (1½ sticks) unsalted butter, room temperature
- ½ cup dry breadcrumbs
- 2 tablespoons Pernod or other anise-flavored liqueur
- 1 teaspoon fennel seeds, ground
- 1 teaspoon hot pepper sauce

- 1 pound (about) rock salt
- 24 fresh oysters, shucked, shells reserved
- ¼ cup freshly grated Parmesan cheese

Position rack in top third of oven and preheat to 450°F. Finely chop garlic in processor. Add spinach, watercress and green onions to garlic. Process, using on/off turns, until mixture is finely chopped. Transfer mixture to medium bowl.

Combine butter, breadcrumbs, Pernod, fennel and hot sauce in processor. Process until well blended. Return spinach mixture to processor. Process, using on/off turns, just until mixtures are blended. Season to taste with salt and pepper. *(Can be made 8 hours ahead. Cover and refrigerate.)*

Sprinkle rock salt over large baking sheet to depth of ½ inch. Arrange oysters in half shells atop rock salt. Top each oyster with 1 tablespoon spinach mixture. Sprinkle with cheese. Bake until spinach mixture browns on top, about 8 minutes.

8 FIRST-COURSE SERVINGS

new at the market

Hershey's chocolate bars (1900)

Wesson Oil (1900)

Barnum's Animal Crackers by Nabisco (1902)

Karo corn syrup (1902)

Canned corn and peas from Minnesota Valley Canning Co., renamed Green Giant in 1925 (1903)

Dole canned pineapple (1903)

Pepsi Cola (1903)

Campbell's Pork & Beans (1904)

Dr Pepper (1904)

French's mustard (1904)

Gold Medal flour sold in small consumer-size bags rather than in bulk (1905)

Hebrew National frankfurters (1905)

Ovaltine (1905)

Royal Crown Cola (1905)

A.1. Steak Sauce (1906)

Kellogg's Corn Flakes (1906)

Canada Dry Ginger Ale (1907)

Hershey's Kisses (1907)

Southwest-Style Salisbury Steaks

Dr. James Henry Salisbury might have been the first of the protein-diet doctors, proclaiming in 1888 that humankind's maladies were caused by too much starchy food. His solution? Chopped lean meat, or hamburger steak. To hide the "liver-y" taste of hamburger, he added horseradish, mustard or Worcestershire sauce. By the 1900s, Salisbury steak was a staple menu item, often served with mushroom gravy or smothered in onions. This version was inspired by today's southwestern cooking.

- 1½ pounds ground chuck beef
- ½ cup shredded Monterey Jack cheese
- ¼ cup chopped fresh cilantro
- 1 4-ounce can chopped mild green chilies
- 2 tablespoons minced green onions
- 1 tablespoon tequila
- 2 teaspoons chili powder
- 1 teaspoon salt

- 1 avocado, pitted, peeled, sliced
- Lime-pickled Red Onions (see recipe below)
- Purchased salsas

Using hands, gently mix first 8 ingredients in large bowl just until blended. Form into four ¾-inch-thick oval patties. *(Can be made 1 day ahead. Cover; chill.)*

Prepare barbecue (medium-high heat). Grill patties until cooked to desired doneness, about 6 minutes per side for medium-rare.

Transfer patties to plates. Top with avocado slices and Lime-pickled Red Onions. Serve, passing salsas alongside.

4 SERVINGS

Lime-pickled Red Onions

- 1 large red onion, thinly sliced
- ¼ cup fresh lime juice
- 2 tablespoons chopped fresh cilantro
- 2 teaspoons olive oil
- ½ teaspoon dried oregano
- ½ teaspoon salt

Mix all ingredients in large bowl. Cover onions and let stand 1 to 3 hours. *(Can be made 2 days ahead. Cover and chill.)*

MAKES ABOUT 2 CUPS

the candy man

Can you imagine making a trip to any candy counter without seeing a Hershey's chocolate bar? An icon to chocolate lovers, that glossy brown-paper-wrapped bar of milk chocolate got its start in 1900 when Milton Hershey sold his Lancaster Caramel Co. for $1 million in cash. As part of the sale, Hershey retained a portion of the old factory that contained chocolate-making equipment. That same year, he introduced the first Hershey's chocolate bars. In 1901, sales totaled $622,000.

Two years later, Hershey began construction of his own factory in Derry Church, Pennsylvania. But he did not simply open a factory: He started an industry—before the mass-produced Hershey's chocolate bar was available, milk chocolate was enjoyed only by the upper classes.

The factory began chocolate production in 1905, and by that time Hershey had several hundred workers on staff. By 1906, the town, which Hershey had helped develop, was renamed Hershey, and the man (and his chocolate) went on to make the sweetest kind of history.

French 75 Cocktail

This intoxicating Champagne cocktail was named after a French 75-millimeter gun used in World War I. Many American bartenders claimed to have invented the drink. One recipe, from 1919, called for absinthe, Calvados and gin, but no Champagne. Supposedly, the Champagne version was introduced at Harry's New York Bar in Paris in 1925. Or the cocktail might have originated with American soldiers in Paris, who added gin and liqueur to Champagne to crank up its potency.

6 tablespoons gin
¼ cup Cointreau or triple sec
1¼ teaspoons fresh lemon juice
6 thin strips lemon peel (yellow part only)
1 750-ml bottle chilled brut Champagne

Mix first 3 ingredients in measuring cup. Divide among 6 Champagne glasses. Add 1 lemon strip to each. Fill with Champagne.

6 SERVINGS

Five-Spice Apple Pie

By the time Crisco came out in 1911, apple pies had long been an American classic. But Crisco, the first hydrogenated vegetable shortening, gave cooks a boost. Here was a shelf-stable alternative to perishable butter and lard. While a lot of consumers were skeptical of Crisco, many early sales were generated by Orthodox Jews, who bought the shortening after a recipe booklet was published in Yiddish showing how Crisco could be used without breaking kosher dietary laws. Its success was assured when rationing made lard scarce during World War I.

CRUST
2 cups all purpose flour
2 tablespoons sugar
¾ teaspoon salt
⅔ cup chilled solid vegetable shortening, cut into ½-inch pieces
6 tablespoons (about) ice water

new at the market

Aunt Jemima Pancake Flour (1910)

Mazola cooking oil, first corn oil sold for home use (1911)

GooGoo Clusters (1912)

Hellmann's Blue Ribbon Mayonnaise (1912)

Lorna Doones (1912)

Oreos (1912)

Life Savers, circular peppermint candies "for that stormy breath" (1913)

Quaker Puffed Rice, Puffed Wheat and the new slogan "Shot from guns," which increased Quaker sales thirty-fold (1913)

Tastykakes (1914)

Kellogg's 40% Bran Flakes (1915)

Clark Bar (1917)

Marshmallow Fluff (1917)

Moon Pie (1917)

Contadina tomato sauce (1918)

I-Scream-Bar, first ice cream bar on a stick and the forerunner to Eskimo Pie (1919)

Kellogg's All Bran (1919)

Malt-O-Meal (1919)

FILLING

- 5 pounds Golden Delicious apples, peeled, cored, cut into ½-inch-thick slices
- 2 tablespoons fresh lemon juice
- 6 tablespoons (¾ stick) unsalted butter
- 1 cup (packed) golden brown sugar
- 2 tablespoons all purpose flour
- 1¼ teaspoons Chinese five-spice powder*

- 2 tablespoons whipping cream
- ½ teaspoon sugar

FOR CRUST: Mix first 3 ingredients in large bowl. Add shortening; cut in using pastry blender or 2 knives until mixture resembles coarse meal with a few pea-size pieces. Mix in enough ice water by tablespoonfuls to form moist clumps. Gather dough into ball. Divide into 2 pieces, 1 slightly larger than the other. Flatten each into disk. Wrap each disk in plastic; refrigerate at least 1 hour. *(Can be made 1 day ahead. Keep refrigerated. Let dough soften slightly at room temperature before rolling out.)*

FOR FILLING: Toss apples and lemon juice in large bowl. Melt butter in heavy large pot over medium heat. Add apples and brown sugar; cook until apples are just tender, stirring occasionally, about 15 minutes. Using slotted spoon, return apples to same bowl. Boil juices in pot until thick, about 15 minutes. Pour juices over apples; cool completely. Mix in flour and five-spice powder.

Position rack in lowest third of oven; preheat to 375°F. Place baking sheet on rack. Roll out larger dough disk on floured surface to 12-inch round. Transfer to 9-inch glass pie dish; trim overhang to 1 inch, if necessary. Spoon filling into crust. Roll out smaller dough disk to 10-inch round. Drape over filling. Press top and bottom edges of dough together; crimp decoratively. Cut small hole in center of crust. Brush crust with cream. Sprinkle with ½ teaspoon sugar.

Place pie on baking sheet in oven; bake until crust is golden brown and filling bubbles thickly, about 1 hour 5 minutes. Transfer pie to rack and cool. Serve slightly warm or at room temperature.

**Available in the spice section of most supermarkets.*

6 TO 8 SERVINGS

the original supermarket sweep

In the early part of the century, grocery shopping was a time-consuming process. A shopper would hand a list to a clerk, who would retrieve the items from shelves or a storeroom. Customers had little, if any, choice about what they were buying.

Change began in 1912, when John and George Hartford established the first A&P "Economy Store." A clerk still took orders, but the store did not offer credit or delivery—a development that spawned the term *cash-and-carry*.

That same year, another market revolution was happening in California, where Alpha Beta Food Market, Ward's Grocerteria and Bay Cities Mercantile originated the *self-service* grocery store.

In Memphis, businessman Clarence Saunders combined the trends in 1916, when he began the Piggly Wiggly chain. Customers followed a serpentine route leading past all 600-plus items on the shelves (a huge selection for the time, though today's markets stock approximately 30,000 items), and sales were rung up at checkout stands. The way was paved for the importance of packaging, brand identity and advertising.

new at the market

Baby Ruth (1920)

Oh Henry! (1920)

Wonder Bread (1920)

Quaker Quick-Cooking Oats (1921)

Mounds Bar (1922)

Almond Roca (1923)

Milky Way (1923)

Reese's Peanut Butter Cups (1923)

Sanka decaffeinated coffee (1923)

Welch's grape jelly (1923)

Yoo-Hoo chocolate drink (1923)

Popsicles (1924)

Wheaties (1924)

Mr. Goodbar (1925)

Hormel canned ham (1926)

Milk Duds (1926)

Hostess Cakes (1927)

Kool-Aid (1927)

Butterfinger (1928)

Peter Pan Peanut Butter (1928)

Rice Krispies (1928)

Velveeta (1928)

Roasted Clams with Pancetta and Red Bell Pepper Coulis

In 1917, a society grande dame asked Julius Keller, maître d' of the Casino restaurant in New York, to surprise her with a new dish. Keller presented clams baked on the half shell, topped with minced bell pepper, herb butter and bacon. By the twenties, Clams Casino, as Keller called it, was ubiquitous on restaurant menus. Here is a lightened version with great lively flavors.

1 large red bell pepper
1 tablespoon olive oil
1 teaspoon dried oregano
1 garlic clove, peeled

24 littleneck clams, scrubbed

3 slices pancetta or bacon, cut into 24 pieces
Lemon wedges

Char bell pepper over gas flame or in broiler until blackened on all sides. Enclose in paper bag; let stand 10 minutes. Peel, seed and coarsely chop bell pepper. Transfer to processor. Add olive oil, dried oregano and garlic clove; puree until smooth. Season coulis to taste with salt and pepper.

Preheat oven to 500°F. Line large baking sheet with foil. Arrange clams on sheet. Bake until clams open, about 6 minutes (discard any that do not open). Cool slightly. Remove top shells; discard, leaving clams in half shells on sheet.

Preheat broiler. Top each clam with 1 teaspoon coulis, then 1 pancetta piece. Broil clams until coulis bubbles and pancetta browns, about 3 minutes. Transfer to platter. Garnish with lemon; serve.

4 APPETIZER SERVINGS

Spaghetti with Sicilian Meatballs

Americans enjoyed most of the food at the scores of Italian restaurants that opened in the twenties, but they couldn't understand spaghetti and tomato sauce: Where was the meat? To accommodate, the restaurants began to top the pasta with meatballs. This takes the dish a step further by adding the Sicilian flavors of pine nuts and currants.

SAUCE

2 tablespoons olive oil
1½ cups chopped onions
2 garlic cloves, minced
2 28-ounce cans diced tomatoes in juice
4 tablespoons chopped fresh basil

MEATBALLS

⅔ cup fresh breadcrumbs
3 tablespoons milk
⅓ cup freshly grated Parmesan cheese
¼ cup finely chopped onion
3 tablespoons chopped fresh basil
1 large egg
1 garlic clove, minced
¼ teaspoon ground black pepper
1 pound sweet Italian sausages, casings removed
2 tablespoons pine nuts, toasted
2 tablespoons dried currants
1 pound spaghetti

FOR SAUCE: Heat oil in heavy large pot over medium-low heat. Add onions; sauté until golden, about 10 minutes. Add garlic; stir 1 minute. Add tomatoes with juices and 2 tablespoons basil; bring to boil. Reduce heat; simmer until sauce thickens, breaking up tomatoes with fork, about 1 hour. Mix in 2 tablespoons basil.

FOR MEATBALLS: Preheat oven to 350°F. Lightly oil baking sheet. Mix crumbs and milk in medium bowl; let stand 5 minutes. Mix in Parmesan, onion, basil, egg, garlic and pepper. Add sausage, pine nuts and currants; blend well. Using wet hands, form mixture into 1¼-inch balls. Place on baking sheet. Bake until meatballs are light brown and cooked through, about 30 minutes. Add to sauce.

Cook spaghetti in large pot of boiling salted water until just tender but still firm to bite. Drain. Mound in dish. Bring sauce and meatballs to simmer. Spoon over spaghetti.

4 TO 6 SERVINGS

the modern kitchen

Imagine life without a refrigerator, pop-up toaster, and gas or electric range. Before the twenties, that was a cook's life. Thankfully, during this roaring decade such appliances became more widely available and more affordable.

Refrigerators (with small freezer sections) gradually took the place of iceboxes. In 1920, only 10,000 refrigerators were sold; by 1929, annual sales had risen to 800,000. Companies promoted the use of their appliances by publishing recipe pamphlets and booklets. General Electric's *Electric Refrigerator Recipes and Menus* included a recipe for frozen cheese salad (a cream cheese, whipped cream and mayonnaise mold that was turned out and served with more mayonnaise).

At the same time, gas ranges began to replace wood-burning stoves in most homes, and pop-up toasters—aside from quickly doing the job—were just plain fun. These new appliances gave women (many of whom had entered the workforce after World War I) some much-needed help in the kitchen. This was the true beginning of the convenience age: Clarence Birdseye's frozen vegetables were on the horizon.

Baked Artichokes with Crab and Sourdough Stuffing

new at the market

Hostess Twinkies (1930)

Snickers (1930)

Bisquick (1931)

Fritos corn chips (1932)

Skippy Peanut Butter (1932)

Campbell's Chicken Noodle and Cream of Mushroom soups (1933)

Ritz Crackers (1934)

Five Flavors Life Savers (1935)

Kraft Miracle Whip dressing (1935)

Kix cereal (1937)

Kraft Macaroni & Cheese Dinner (1937)

Pepperidge Farm bread (1937)

Spam (1937)

Lawry's Seasoned Salt (1938)

Lay's potato chips (1938)

Nestlé Crunch bar (1938)

Artichokes, an Old World food, came to America with Italian immigrants and found a happy home in the near-Mediterranean climate of California. As "ethnic" fare, artichokes took their time catching on outside the Golden State. They finally did in the thirties and became something of a fad. Artichokes were not limited to the vegetable course, either. Sometimes the center "choke" was scooped out and the hollow filled with a stuffing for a fashionable light lunch entrée.

6 tablespoons (¾ stick) butter
1 cup finely chopped red bell pepper
¾ cup finely chopped onion
2 celery stalks, finely chopped
8 garlic cloves, minced
3 cups fresh breadcrumbs made from crustless sourdough bread
8 ounces crabmeat

4 large artichokes (each about 1 pound)

Melt butter in heavy medium skillet over medium heat. Add bell pepper, onion, celery and garlic. Sauté until onion is translucent, about 6 minutes. Transfer to large bowl and cool completely. Mix in breadcrumbs and crabmeat. Season stuffing with salt and pepper. *(Can be made 1 day ahead. Cover and refrigerate.)*

Preheat oven to 375°F. Cut off top third of each artichoke; discard. Cut off stem. Pull out yellow and small purple-tipped leaves from center. Using melon baller, scoop out fibrous choke.

Gently pull leaves outward from center until leaves open slightly. Pack stuffing into each artichoke cavity and between first and second center layers of leaves, mounding slightly. Place artichokes in 13 x 9 x 2-inch baking dish. Add enough water to come ¾ inch up sides of dish. Cover with foil. Bake artichokes until outer leaf pulls away easily, about 1 hour 15 minutes.

4 SERVINGS

Three-Cheese Pasta Gratin with Almond Crust

Even lean, mean Depression-era macaroni and cheese was comforting, a tribute to the twin powers of carbohydrates and melted cheese, which are just as irresistible now as they were then. Some fans love the crunchy crust while others crave the creamy center. This lush and ultra-tangy millennium mac and cheese aims to please adherents of both schools of thought.

3 tablespoons butter
1 garlic clove, pressed
3 tablespoons all purpose flour
4 cups hot whole milk
10 ounces extra-sharp cheddar cheese, grated (about 3 cups)
8 ounces hot pepper Monterey Jack cheese, grated (about 2½ cups)
1⅔ cups lightly packed grated Parmesan cheese
1 teaspoon hot pepper sauce

½ cup whole almonds
¼ cup fine dry breadcrumbs

1 pound short tube-shaped pasta (such as cavatapi or macaroni)

Melt butter in heavy medium saucepan over medium heat. Add garlic; sauté until fragrant, about 1 minute. Add flour; stir 3 minutes. Whisk in hot milk. Bring to simmer, stirring. Cover partially; simmer until sauce thickens slightly, stirring occasionally, about 8 minutes. Remove from heat. Add cheddar and Jack cheeses, 1⅓ cups Parmesan cheese and hot pepper sauce. Whisk until sauce is smooth. Season with salt and pepper. *(Can be made 1 day ahead. Cover; chill. Whisk over medium heat to rewarm before using.)*

Preheat oven to 400°F. Generously butter bottom and sides of 13 x 9 x 2-inch baking dish. Blend ⅓ cup Parmesan, almonds and breadcrumbs in processor until nuts are coarsely ground. Add ½ cup almond mixture to prepared dish. Tilt dish to coat bottom and sides. Return any loose almond mixture to processor.

Cook pasta in large pot of boiling salted water until tender. Drain well. Return pasta to pot. Add sauce; stir to coat. Transfer to prepared dish. Sprinkle remaining almond mixture over.

Bake until almond mixture is golden and crunchy and sauce bubbles, about 30 minutes. Cool on rack 5 minutes.

8 SERVINGS

route 66: the mother road

When U.S. Highway 66 was completed in 1938, it became a vital 2,450-mile artery between Chicago and Los Angeles, snaking its way westward through eight states. Route 66, as it was called, was unlike many straight-as-an-arrow highways because it didn't bypass rural communities; instead it climbed north and dipped south to pass right through them in an effort to link small-town America with larger metropolitan areas.

With Route 66, farmers had a pipeline for shipping their food to the big cities. And for the thousands who fled the effects of the Dust Bowl, there were gas stations, motels and quick-stop stores dotting the roadside to take care of their needs.

Chain restaurants also flourished on Route 66. Steak 'n Shake, for example, first served its steakburgers, milk shakes and shoestring french fries in 1934 in Normal, Illinois. As more Steak 'n Shake restaurants opened along the scenic route, customers were happy to see a familiar name in an unfamiliar location.

It was just the beginning of a whole new way of dining out.

Victory Garden Chicken-Vegetable Soup

Throughout World War II, everyone who had even a little plot of land was encouraged to grow a vegetable garden. Back then, this comforting soup would most frequently be made from water and contain no chicken, which was a Sunday treat. For convenience, you can skip the first part of this recipe and use six cups of stock or canned broth and omit the chicken altogether. But if you want to make the stock from scratch, be sure to do so a day ahead.

- 1 3½-pound chicken, cut into 8 pieces
- 8 cups water
- ¾ cup dry white wine
- 2 teaspoons salt

- 2 teaspoons olive oil
- 1 medium onion, finely chopped
- 1 pound red-skinned potatoes, peeled, cut into ½-inch pieces
- 1 pound tomatoes, coarsely chopped
- 3 medium carrots, peeled, sliced
- 4 ounces green beans, trimmed, cut into 1-inch pieces
- 2 medium zucchini, trimmed, cut into ½-inch pieces
- 1 cup fresh or frozen corn kernels
- 2 cups (packed) thinly sliced fresh spinach leaves
- ⅓ cup thinly sliced fresh basil

Bring chicken, 8 cups water, wine and 1 teaspoon salt to boil in large pot, skimming surface. Cover; simmer until chicken is cooked through, about 25 minutes. Transfer chicken breast and thigh pieces to platter (leave remaining chicken and stock in pot). Remove meat from bones; cut into ½-inch pieces. Cover and chill meat. Return scraps and bones to pot.

Cover stock and simmer 1 hour. Strain. Cool stock slightly. Chill overnight. Spoon fat off top and discard.

Heat 2 teaspoons oil in large pot over medium heat. Add onion; sauté until golden, about 6 minutes. Add stock and bring to

new at the market

M&Ms (1941)

Maytag Blue cheese (1941)

Dannon yogurt (1942)

La Choy canned Chinese foods (1942)

Chiquita bananas (1944)

Cheerios (1945)

French's instant mashed potatoes (1946)

Maxwell House instant coffee (1946)

Minute Maid frozen orange juice (1946)

Ragú spaghetti sauce (1946)

Reddi-wip (1947)

Reynolds Wrap aluminum foil (1947)

Cheetos (1948)

Nestlé's Quik (1948)

V8 juice (1948)

Pillsbury and General Mills cake mixes (1949)

Sara Lee Cheesecake (1949)

boil. Add potatoes, tomatoes, carrots, green beans and 1 teaspoon salt. Simmer 10 minutes. Add zucchini and corn; simmer until vegetables are tender, about 15 minutes. Stir in spinach and chicken meat. Simmer until chicken is heated through, about 3 minutes. Stir in basil. Season with salt and pepper.

6 TO 8 SERVINGS

Chocolate Chunk and Pecan Cookies

In 1933, Ruth Wakefield of the Toll House Inn in Whitman, Massachusetts, chopped up some chocolate bars and added the chunks to cookie dough, hoping that they would blend into the dough as they melted. Instead they held their shape, and Toll House cookies were a delicious creation. By the 1940s they were a hit.

- 1 cup all purpose flour
- ½ teaspoon ground cinnamon
- ½ teaspoon baking soda
- ¼ teaspoon salt
- ½ cup butter, room temperature
- ¾ cup (packed) golden brown sugar
- 1½ teaspoons vanilla extract
- ¼ teaspoon almond extract
- 1 large egg
- 1 cup coarsely chopped pecans
- 6 ounces semisweet chocolate, coarsely chopped

Preheat oven to 350°F. Mix first 4 ingredients in medium bowl. Using electric mixer, beat butter, brown sugar, and vanilla and almond extracts in large bowl until blended. Add egg; beat until fluffy. Beat in flour mixture. Stir pecans and chocolate pieces into dough.

Using 2 tablespoonfuls dough for each cookie, drop dough mounds onto ungreased baking sheets, spacing 2 inches apart. Press down on tops slightly to flatten.

Bake cookies until edges begin to brown but centers are still soft, about 13 minutes. Let cool on sheets 2 minutes. Transfer cookies to racks; cool completely. *(Can be made 2 days ahead. Store in airtight container at room temperature.)*

MAKES ABOUT 1½ DOZEN

short rations

In May 1942—when food and gas rationing took effect—the war really hit home. Sugar was the first to be rationed (eight ounces per person per week); soon to follow were coffee, canned foods, meat, fish, butter and cheese.

The system was complicated. Everyone was issued a ration book with red and blue coupons of different values. Each family member was allotted 48 blue points and 64 red points per month, or about two pounds of canned fruit and vegetables, twenty-eight ounces of meat and four ounces of cheese. New ration books were issued monthly, at which time the old coupons became unusable. As a result, budgeting and grocery shopping took up much of a housewife's day.

There were, of course, various ways to supplement the ration books. Many people had Victory gardens, and there was a thriving black market, which ranged from the butcher who held back a nice cut of meat for a certain special customer to the rustler who stole cattle.

Rationing didn't last long, though. By the end of the decade, America was entering one of the greatest periods of abundance ever known.

new at the market

Kraft pre-sliced processed cheese (1950)
Sugar Pops (1950)
Rice Chex and Wheat Chex (1950)
Duncan Hines Cake Mix (1951)
Kellogg's Sugar Frosted Flakes (1952)
Lipton onion soup mix (1952)
Mrs. Paul's Frozen Fish Sticks (1952)
Cheez Whiz (1953)
Eggos frozen waffles (1953)
Kellogg's Sugar Smacks (1953)
Lawry's Original Spaghetti Sauce Mix (1953)
Carnation's instant nonfat dry milk (1954)
M&M's peanut chocolate candies (1954)
Trix (1954)
Pepperidge Farm cookies (1955)
Imperial margarine (1956)
Sweet 'n Low (1957)
Chicken Ramen (1958)
Cocoa Krispies (1958)
Cocoa Puffs (1958)
Corn Chex (1958)
Jif Peanut Butter (1958)
Rice-a-Roni (1958)
Häagen-Dazs (1959)
Tang (1959)

Tuna and Vegetable Fettuccine with Lemon Breadcrumbs

Both easy and inexpensive, tuna-noodle casserole stretched proteins and carbohydrates to the limits and fed at least a generation of American kids very well. Canned tuna will never go away, but fresh tuna has joined it as a culinary staple, and it stars in this deconstructed version of the classic. All the elements that make tuna casserole so appealing and comforting are here, just slightly rearranged. And there's no need to serve this on a cafeteria tray: It's good enough for your best china.

- 7 tablespoons butter
- 1 tablespoon grated lemon peel
- 2 cups fresh breadcrumbs

- 2 cups whipping cream
- 8 ounces cherry tomatoes, halved
- 1 cup frozen petite peas, thawed
- 1 pound fresh tuna, cut into ½-inch pieces

- 1 pound fresh fettuccine
- 1 cup freshly grated Parmesan cheese
- 2 tablespoons minced fresh parsley

Melt 4 tablespoons butter in heavy medium skillet over medium heat. Add lemon peel; sauté 1 minute. Add breadcrumbs; sauté until golden, about 5 minutes. Season with salt and pepper.

Combine cream, tomatoes, peas and 3 tablespoons butter in large deep skillet. Simmer over medium heat until sauce begins to thicken, about 3 minutes. Add tuna and simmer until tuna is cooked through, about 3 minutes. Season to taste with salt and pepper.

Meanwhile, cook pasta in large pot of boiling salted water until just tender. Drain. Add pasta, cheese and parsley to sauce; toss. Season to taste with salt and pepper.

Divide pasta among plates. Sprinkle with lemon breadcrumbs and then serve immediately.

6 SERVINGS

Coffee Baked Alaska with Mocha Sauce

Invented in the 1800s, baked Alaska was possibly named to commemorate America's purchase of that northern territory. The dessert was a big hit in the fifties because convenience was a watchword, and for all the showy effect it created at the table, baked Alaska was not difficult to make. These days, store-bought premium ice creams make the dessert taste even better and offer a wide range of flavor options.

CAKE

1 quart coffee ice cream, softened
1 10.75-ounce frozen pound cake

4 large egg whites
¼ teaspoon cream of tartar
1 teaspoon coffee liqueur
⅓ cup sugar

SAUCE

1½ cups freshly brewed strong coffee
10 ounces semisweet chocolate, chopped
2 tablespoons coffee liqueur

FOR CAKE: Line 9 x 5 x 2½-inch metal loaf pan with plastic wrap, leaving overhang. Spoon ice cream into pan, spreading evenly. Cut cake horizontally in half. Arrange 1 cake piece, cut side down, atop ice cream and against 1 corner of pan. Cut remaining cake piece into strips and arrange in pan to cover ice cream completely. Cover with plastic; freeze until firm, at least 4 hours.

Uncover cake. Invert onto metal or other ovenproof platter. Freeze while preparing meringue. Beat egg whites in large bowl until foamy. Add cream of tartar. Beat until soft peaks form. Beat in liqueur. Gradually add sugar, beating until stiff glossy peaks form. Spread meringue over cake, covering cake completely and sealing meringue to platter. Freeze overnight.

FOR SAUCE: Combine coffee and semisweet chocolate in heavy small saucepan. Stir over medium-low heat until mixture is smooth. Increase heat to medium. Simmer until sauce thickens, about 2 minutes. Cool slightly. Stir in coffee liqueur.

Position rack in center of oven and preheat to 500°F for 20 minutes. Bake until meringue is lightly browned and just set, 3 minutes. Cut into slices; arrange on plates. Spoon warm sauce around.

6 TO 8 SERVINGS

couch potatoes

The fifties were television years: Programming and advertising flourished, and so did sales of television sets as they became more affordable. By the end of the decade, in fact, more than 70 percent of American families owned at least one TV. And because everyone was fascinated by the tube, everyone wanted to sit in front of it all the time, including dinnertime.

Swanson's TV dinners, introduced in 1954, helped move dinner from the dining room to the living room. The meal sold for 98 cents, and there was only one kind—gravy-topped sliced turkey with corn bread stuffing, buttered peas and whipped sweet potatoes. The precooked food was packaged in a three-section aluminum tray in a carton with a label that resembled a TV screen (the first cartons even had a channel dial and a simulated wood console). The packaging offered the convenience of no prep work or cleanup—the company touted it as the "most delicious turkey dinner you never had to cook."

Thanks to Swanson, no one had to miss a single second of Uncle Miltie, "I Love Lucy," or any other favorite show.

new at the market

Coffee-Mate (1961)

Sprite (1961)

Total breakfast cereal (1961)

Diet colas sweetened with cyclamates: Diet Rite was first (1962), followed by Tab and Diet Pepsi

Frozen pie crust (1962)

Cremora nondairy creamer (1963)

Carnation Instant Breakfast (1964)

Lucky Charms (1964)

Maxim freeze-dried instant coffee (1964)

Pop-Tarts (1964)

Apple Jacks cereal (1965)

Cool Whip (1965)

Shake 'n' Bake (1965)

Bac*Os (1966)

Kellogg's Product 19 (1966)

$100,000 Bar (1966)

Taster's Choice freeze-dried instant coffee (1966)

Gatorade (1967)

Lawry's Taco Seasoning (1967)

Kellogg's Frosted Mini-Wheats (1969)

Pringles potato chips (1969)

Santa Fe Gazpacho

Many Americans first tasted this cold vegetable soup at the 1964 New York World's Fair. Gazpacho came into favor partly as a vehicle for showing off blenders, the popularity of which created a giant boom in recipes that called for liquefying ingredients. This delicious recipe goes the Spanish classic one better with the addition of smoky *chipotle* chilies.

- 1 11-ounce cucumber, peeled, halved lengthwise, seeded
- 1¼ cups canned low-salt chicken broth or vegetable broth
- 1¼ pounds tomatoes, quartered
- 1 7.25-ounce jar roasted red peppers, drained
- 3 tablespoons chopped fresh cilantro
- 2 tablespoons fresh lime juice
- 2 teaspoons minced canned chipotle chilies*

- 2 large green onions, finely chopped
- ½ avocado, peeled, finely chopped
- ½ cup finely chopped peeled jicama
- ½ cup finely chopped green bell pepper
- ½ cup finely chopped plum tomatoes

Coarsely chop half of cucumber; place in blender. Add ½ cup broth and next 5 ingredients; puree until smooth. Pour soup into large bowl. Mix in ¾ cup broth. Season with salt and pepper. Cover; chill at least 2 hours and up to 6 hours.

Mix 1 rounded tablespoon each of green onions, avocado, jicama, green bell pepper and tomatoes in small bowl; reserve for garnish. Mix remaining green onions, avocado, jicama, bell pepper and chopped tomatoes into soup. Ladle soup into bowls. Sprinkle with reserved garnish and serve.

*Chipotle *chilies canned in a spicy tomato sauce, sometimes called* adobo, *are sold at Latin American markets, specialty foods stores and also at some supermarkets.*

4 SERVINGS

Duck à l'Orange

One of the dishes that introduced Americans to French food. This version calls for duck breasts and a simple reduction sauce flavored with orange.

- ¼ cup sugar
- 2 tablespoons water
- 2 tablespoons Sherry wine vinegar
- 1½ cups fresh orange juice
- 2 tablespoons minced shallots
- 1½ cups canned low-salt chicken broth

- 4 large oranges

- 2 1-pound boneless Muscovy duck breast halves, thawed if frozen

- ¼ cup (½ stick) unsalted butter
- 2 tablespoons grated orange peel

Stir sugar and water in heavy medium saucepan over medium heat until sugar dissolves. Increase heat; boil until syrup turns deep amber, occasionally brushing down sides of pan with wet pastry brush and swirling pan, 8 minutes. Remove from heat. Mix in vinegar (mixture will bubble vigorously). Add juice and shallots; boil until reduced to ½ cup, stirring occasionally, 15 minutes. Add broth; boil until reduced to ¾ cup, 30 minutes. Set aside.

Using small knife, cut off peel and white pith from 4 oranges. Working over bowl, cut between membranes to release segments. *(Sauce and oranges can be prepared 6 hours ahead; chill.)*

Using small knife, score duck skin (do not pierce meat) in crosshatch pattern. Sprinkle duck with salt and pepper. Heat heavy large skillet over medium-high heat. Place duck breasts, skin side down, in skillet. Cook until brown and crisp, about 8 minutes. Turn duck and cook to desired doneness, about 10 minutes longer for medium-rare. Transfer to cutting board. Let stand 10 minutes.

Meanwhile, bring sauce to simmer. Add butter and 1 tablespoon grated orange peel; whisk just until butter melts. Drain orange segments and mix into sauce. Set aside.

Slice duck breasts crosswise on diagonal. Arrange on 4 plates. Spoon orange segments with sauce alongside. Sprinkle with peel.

4 SERVINGS

à la julia

In the 1960s, Americans learned to cook French food, and Julia Child was their teacher. With her distinctive voice and down-to-earth manner, Child rose to national fame as the host of "The French Chef" television series, which followed by one year the publication of volume one of the landmark book *Mastering the Art of French Cooking,* which she co-authored with Simone Beck and Louisette Bertholle.

An unpretentious graduate of the Cordon Bleu cooking school in Paris, the California-born Child was at ease in front of the camera, taking the same delight in her grand goofs as in her perfectly roasted goose, all the while making witty remarks, many at her own expense. Child made haute cuisine approachable, and her show was an instant hit.

While democratizing the most hallowed cuisine in the world, Julia Child sparked significant trends: stylish home entertaining, cooking on television, cookware stores and the phenomenon of chef as celebrity. Along the way she became the best-loved cook of all, a title she still holds.

Hazelnut-crusted Goat Cheese Salad

Alice Waters, who opened Chez Panisse in 1971, took salads to new heights with unusual, farm-fresh greens; she also popularized the use of goat cheese, which was being made by Laura Chenel not far from the Berkeley restaurant. Those ingredients come together in this delicious salad.

- ¼ cup all purpose flour
- ¼ cup plain dry breadcrumbs
- 1 5.5-ounce log soft fresh goat cheese (such as Montrachet), cut into 4 equal rounds, chilled
- 1 large egg, beaten to blend
- 3 tablespoons coarsely chopped hazelnuts

- 1 tablespoon red wine vinegar
- 1 tablespoon grated orange peel
- 1 tablespoon frozen orange juice concentrate, thawed
- ¼ cup olive oil

- 1 large bunch watercress, stems trimmed
- 1 large head Belgian endive, thinly sliced lengthwise

Place flour and breadcrumbs on separate plates. Coat cheese rounds with flour. Dip cheese into egg, then into breadcrumbs, coating completely. Place on small baking sheet. Spoon hazelnuts atop cheese. Gently press hazelnuts into cheese to adhere. Cover and refrigerate at least 30 minutes or overnight.

Whisk vinegar, orange peel and orange juice concentrate in medium bowl to blend. Gradually whisk in oil. Season with salt and pepper. *(Vinaigrette can be made 4 hours ahead. Store at room temperature; rewhisk before using.)*

Preheat oven to 400°F. Bake cheese until heated through and coating browns, about 6 minutes.

Toss watercress and endive in large bowl with enough vinaigrette to coat. Season greens with salt and pepper. Divide greens among 4 plates. Top with warm cheese.

4 FIRST-COURSE SERVINGS

new at the market

Hamburger Helper (1970)

Orville Redenbacher's Gourmet Popping Corn (1970)

Celestial Seasonings Herbal Teas (1971)

Quaker Oats 100% Natural, the first mainstream granola (1972)

Snapple fruit juices (1972)

Cup O'Noodles (1973)

Stove Top Stuffing (1973)

Miller Lite, the first light beer (1974)

Pop Rocks (1974)

Yoplait Yogurt (1974)

Famous Amos Chocolate Chip Cookies (1975)

Perrier (1976)

Starburst fruit chews (1976)

Ben & Jerry's Ice Cream (1978)

Reese's Pieces (1978)

Szechuan Shrimp with Peppers

Nixon's re-establishment of relations with China led Americans to discover, among other things, that there was more to Chinese cooking than the Cantonese dishes we had all grown up with—including the food of the Szechuan province.

- 1 pound uncooked large shrimp, peeled, deveined
- 2 tablespoons dry Sherry
- 1½ tablespoons minced peeled fresh ginger
- 2 garlic cloves, minced
- ½ teaspoon dried crushed red pepper

- ½ cup canned low-salt chicken broth
- 2 teaspoons cornstarch
- 1½ tablespoons soy sauce
- 1 tablespoon Asian chili-garlic sauce
- 1 teaspoon sugar

- 1 tablespoon peanut oil
- 1 red bell pepper, cut into 1-inch diamond-shape pieces
- 6 green onions, cut into ½-inch pieces
- Cooked white rice

Combine first 5 ingredients in large bowl; toss to coat. Cover shrimp and let stand for 30 minutes.

Combine chicken broth and cornstarch in small bowl; stir to dissolve cornstarch. Combine soy sauce, Asian chili-garlic sauce and sugar in another small bowl.

Heat oil in wok or heavy large skillet over medium-high heat. Add bell pepper and stir-fry until slightly softened, about 4 minutes. Add shrimp mixture; stir-fry 2 minutes. Add onions; stir-fry until shrimp are pink, 30 seconds. Mix in soy sauce mixture. Add cornstarch mixture. Cook until sauce is thickened, about 1 minute. Transfer to bowl; serve immediately with rice.

4 SERVINGS

the new cooking

La nouvelle cuisine was given its name in the October 1973 issue of *Gault-Millau*, a French magazine headed up by food writers Henri Gault and Christian Millau. Translated as "the new cooking," the term was intended to capture a style that had been developing in France for several years, one that was moving away from the restrictions of classical cooking and toward greater simplicity, lightness and freshness. Chefs like Paul Bocuse and Roger Vergé broke from tradition and devised their own cuisine, using new methods and techniques and creating entirely new dishes.

And it wasn't just French chefs who were paying attention. The movement quickly took hold on this side of the Atlantic, with talents like Jean Banchet and Jean Bertranou experimenting with their own interpretations of the new cooking.

By the mid-eighties, the word *nouvelle* came to connote a dish that was overly stylized, preciously presented and very expensive. Its moment of fame may have passed, but many of its tenets live on.

Duck Sausage Pizza with Green Onions and Tomato

Wolfgang Puck gets the credit for redefining pizza at his trend-setting Spago restaurant in West Hollywood. The inventive pizzas came topped with everything from goat cheese and Black Forest ham to artichokes and exotic mushrooms. Duck sausage pizzas, like this one, were a real hit.

new at the market

Fruit Roll-Ups (1980)

Lean Cuisine frozen dinners (1981)

Tofutti frozen dessert (1981)

Bud Light (1982)

Mrs. Butterworth's Pancake Mix (1982)

Scramblers (1982)

Chewy Chips Ahoy cookies (1984)

Hidden Valley "ranch" dressing (1984)

Alpine White candy bar (1985)

Pop Secret Microwave Popcorn (1986)

Campbell's Special Request soups (1987)

Snapple bottled iced tea (1987)

Boboli pizza crusts (1988)

- 1 tablespoon extra-virgin olive oil
- 2 garlic cloves, minced
- ⅛ teaspoon dried crushed red pepper
- 1 10-ounce fully baked thin pizza crust (such as Boboli)
- 1½ cups (packed) grated mozzarella cheese (about 6 ounces)
- ½ cup chopped tomato
- ½ teaspoon dried oregano
- 2 smoked duck, chicken or turkey sausages, sliced
- ⅓ cup finely chopped green onions
- ½ cup freshly grated Parmesan cheese (about 1½ ounces)

Minced fresh parsley

Position rack in center of oven and preheat to 450°F. Mix olive oil, minced garlic and dried crushed red pepper in small bowl. Place pizza crust on rimless baking sheet. Sprinkle grated mozzarella cheese over all but 1-inch border of crust. Top mozzarella with chopped tomato, then oregano, sliced sausages, chopped green onions and freshly grated Parmesan cheese, in that order. Drizzle garlic-oil mixture over pizza.

Bake pizza until crust edges are crisp and brown and cheese melts, about 15 minutes. Sprinkle pizza with minced fresh parsley. Cut pizza into wedges and then serve immediately.

4 SERVINGS

Bittersweet Chocolate and Hazelnut Truffles

Alice Medrich, founder of the Berkeley chocolate shop Cocolat, is credited with starting the craze for these intense little nuggets.

8 ounces bittersweet (not unsweetened) or semisweet chocolate, chopped
½ cup plus 2 tablespoons whipping cream
1 tablespoon brandy
¼ teaspoon vanilla extract

6 tablespoons ground toasted hazelnuts

1½ cups hazelnuts, toasted, chopped

Place chocolate in medium metal bowl. Bring cream to simmer in small saucepan. Pour over chocolate; let stand 2 minutes. Whisk until smooth. Mix in brandy and vanilla. Cool completely, stirring occasionally, about 30 minutes.

Using electric mixer, beat chocolate mixture until fluffy and lighter in color, about 4 minutes. Mix in 6 tablespoons ground hazelnuts. Cover and refrigerate truffle mixture until firm, about 2 hours.

Line baking sheet with waxed paper. Place 1½ cups chopped nuts in another medium bowl. Fill glass with hot water. Dip 1-inch-diameter melon baller into water, then into truffle mixture, forming round truffle. Drop truffle into nuts; roll to coat completely and press to adhere. Place on prepared sheet. Repeat with remaining truffle mixture and nuts. Cover and chill until firm, about 1 hour. *(Can be made 2 days ahead; keep chilled.)*

MAKES ABOUT 2½ DOZEN

the local fare

What Alice Waters started at Chez Panisse in the seventies—namely, a style of cooking based on the freshest ingredients—came to be called "California cuisine" in the eighties. And the success of that style spawned a rush to other regional cuisines from coast to coast. Wherever people went, be it the Southwest, New England, Hawaii, the Pacific Northwest or the Midwest, there would be chefs reinventing the local fare.

Some versions of regional cooking stand out. Alice Waters and her Southern California counterparts, Michael McCarty and Wolfgang Puck, crafted menus of creative food that changed the course of cooking in this century.

Southwestern food got its start and was propelled into the mainstream by its most talented practitioners: Mark Miller, Dean Fearing and Stephan Pyles.

It took just one big man, one Paul Prudhomme, to single-handedly ignite the Cajun craze. He did it with blackened redfish. The dish's popularity dwindled by decade's end, but much of what was good about regional cooking is as delicious today as it ever was.

Wild Mushroom Risotto

new at the market

Stouffer's Homestyle entrées (1991)

AriZona bottled iced tea (1992)

Charlie's Lunch Kit from StarKist (1992)

Nestea bottled iced tea (1992)

Prego Pizza Sauce (1992)

Boca Burger (1993)

Harvest Burger (1993)

Progresso Healthy Classics Soups (1993)

Promise Ultra nonfat margarine (1993)

SnackWell's cookies and crackers (1993)

Fruitopia drinks (1994)

Healthy Choice breakfast cereals (1994)

DiGiorno Rising Crust Pizza (1995)

Lay's Baked Potato Crisps (1996)

V8 Splash (1997)

Frito-Lay Wow! chips (1998)

Kellogg's Smart Start cereal (1998)

Kellogg's Snack Pack cereals (1998)

Hershey's Bites (1999)

Popular in the Italian kitchen for eons, risotto and wild mushrooms were embraced in the nineties by American home cooks and restaurant chefs alike. Offer this delicious version as a starter or a main course.

5 cups canned low-salt chicken broth
½ ounce dried porcini mushrooms,* rinsed

2 tablespoons (¼ stick) butter
1 tablespoon extra-virgin olive oil
2½ cups finely chopped onions
12 ounces crimini mushrooms, finely chopped
2 large garlic cloves, minced
1 tablespoon minced fresh thyme
1 tablespoon minced fresh marjoram
1½ cups arborio rice or medium-grain white rice
½ cup dry white wine
½ cup grated Parmesan cheese
Additional grated Parmesan cheese

Bring broth to simmer in heavy medium saucepan. Add porcini and simmer until just tender, about 2 minutes. Using slotted spoon, transfer mushrooms to plate. Cool mushrooms and chop finely. Cover broth and keep warm over very low heat.

Melt butter with oil in heavy large saucepan over medium heat. Add onions; sauté until tender, about 10 minutes. Add crimini mushrooms; sauté until tender, about 8 minutes. Add porcini, garlic and both herbs; sauté 4 minutes. Add rice; stir 2 minutes. Add wine; cook until liquid is absorbed, stirring often, about 3 minutes. Add 1 cup hot broth; simmer until liquid is absorbed, stirring often, about 8 minutes. Continue to cook until rice is just tender and mixture is creamy, adding more broth by cupfuls and stirring often, about 30 minutes. Mix in ½ cup cheese. Season with salt and pepper. Serve, passing additional cheese separately.

**Available at Italian markets and many supermarkets.*

6 FIRST-COURSE OR 4 MAIN-COURSE SERVINGS

Rosemary Focaccia with Olives

Over the past few years, the popular Italian flatbread has made its way into bread baskets at home and in restaurants. This version is tender and redolent of rosemary. It's perfect as a snack, served with soup and salad, or split for sandwiches.

1 12- to 16-ounce russet potato

2½ cups (or more) bread flour
3 teaspoons fresh rosemary leaves
1 teaspoon salt
1 cup warm water (105°F to 115°F)
¼ teaspoon sugar
1 envelope dry yeast
4 tablespoons extra-virgin olive oil

12 oil-cured black olives, pitted, halved
½ teaspoon coarse sea salt

Pierce potato several times with fork. Microwave on high until tender, turning once, about 12 minutes. Cut in half. Scoop flesh into small bowl; mash well. Measure ⅔ cup (packed) mashed potato; cool.

Combine 2½ cups flour, half of rosemary and 1 teaspoon salt in processor; blend until rosemary is chopped, about 1 minute. Add potato; blend in, using about 25 on/off turns. Combine 1 cup warm water and sugar in 2-cup glass measuring cup; sprinkle yeast over. Let stand until foamy, about 5 minutes. Stir 3 tablespoons oil into yeast mixture. With processor running, pour yeast mixture into flour mixture. Process until smooth, about 1 minute. Scrape dough out onto lightly floured surface. Knead until dough feels silky, sprinkling with more flour as needed, about 1 minute. Place dough in large oiled bowl; turn to coat. Cover with towel; let rise in warm area until doubled in volume, about 1 hour.

Position rack in center of oven and preheat to 450°F. Brush large baking sheet with oil. Punch down dough; knead 30 seconds on lightly floured surface. Stretch or pat out dough to 12-inch round. Transfer round to prepared baking sheet. Press dough all over with fingertips to dimple. Brush with 1 tablespoon oil. Press olive halves, cut side down, into dough. Sprinkle with sea salt. Let rise until just puffy, about 20 minutes. Bake until golden, about 18 minutes. Serve warm or at room temperature.

MAKES ONE 13-INCH ROUND BREAD

america's green acres

As the century drew to a close, Americans looked to their past to rediscover the pleasures of getting back to nature. Cashing in on this desire were farmers' markets: There were just a few hundred in the eighties; by 1998 there were more than 2,700.

The organic foods industry was also a big story. As part of the 1990 Farm Bill, Congress included the Organic Food Production Act, which authorized development of national standards for labeling foods "organic." But in 1997, when the USDA released these long-awaited rules, there was such an outcry against many of the proposed allowances—like the inclusion of genetically altered foods—that the department was flooded with an unprecedented 200,000 angry comments from the general public. The original draft was scrapped, and the process began anew.

But this governmental blunder didn't stop the organic industry's burgeoning sales, because individual states already had their own standards and watchdog agencies in place. The organic industry posted double-digit growth throughout the decade, with sales topping $4 billion.

index

Page numbers in *italics* indicate color photographs.

acknowledgments

The following people contributed the recipes included in this book: Bruce Aidells; Brad Avooske; Melanie Barnard; Jim Botsacos; Georgeanne Brennan; John Brescio; Meg and Paul Brown; Buddakan, Philadelphia, Pennsylvania; Lisa Caiazzo; Carmen and Henri Cauvin; Lauren Chattman; Lane Crowther; Brooke Dojny; Crescent Dragonwagon; Kara and Jeremiah Evarts; Tarla Fallgatter; Barbara Pool Fenzl; Pamela Fitzpatrick; Janet Fletcher; Jim Fobel; Darra Goldstein; Lauren Groveman; Dahlia and Andy Haas; Ken Haedrich; Cheryl Alters Jamison and Bill Jamison; Michele Anna Jordan; Sarah and Paul Keith; Jeanne Thiel Kelley; Elinor Kilvans; La Cabro d'Or, Les Baux-de-Provence, France; La Fanny, Nice, France; Rebecca Levy; Susan Herrmann Loomis; Donata Maggipinto; Michael McLaughlin; Susie and Bruce Meyer; Dorte Lambert-Milman; Jinx and Jefferson Morgan; Selma Brown Morrow; Mark Okumura; Sri Owen; Rochelle Palermo; Christine Piccin; Anita Ravon; Mary Risley; Rick Rodgers; Betty Rosbottom; Martha Rose Shulman; Stacey Siegal; Jeanne Silvestri; Marie Simmons; Prem K. Singh; Sarah Tenaglia; Julian Teixeira; Harriett Tupler; Mary Vaughan; Roger Vergé; Mark Weatherbe; Pat Willard; Colm Wood.

The following people contributed the photographs included in this book: Jack Andersen; Noel Barnhurst; David Bishop; Steve Cohen; Tom Collicott; Wyatt Counts; Julie Dennis; Richard Eskite; Beth Galton; Susan Goines; Laura Johansen; Deborah Klesenski; Michael La Riche; Brian Leatart; Charles Masters; Michael McDermit; Paul Moore; Victoria Pearson; Karl Petzke; David Roth; Jeff Sarpa; Ellen Silverman; Margaret Skinner; Mark Thomas; Georges Vérnon; Stuart Watson.

Front jacket photo: Mark Thomas, Photographer; Dora Jonassen, Food Stylist; Nancy Micklin, Prop Stylist.